PALEO
on a Budget

Saving Money • Eating Healthy

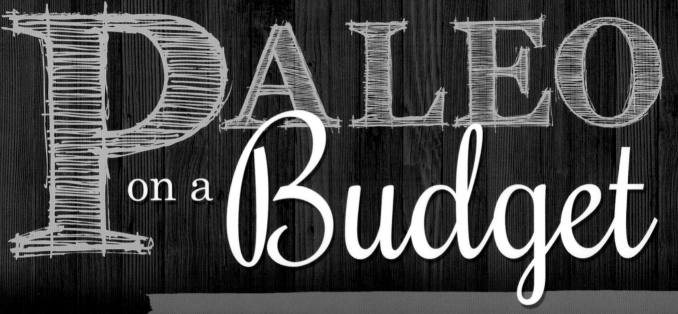

Elizabeth McGaw

Front Table Books
An Imprint of Cedar Fort, Inc. • Springville, Utah

ISBN 13: 978-1-4621-1327-9

Published by Front Table Books, an imprint of Cedar Fort, Inc.
2373 W. 700 S., Springville, UT 84663
Distributed by Cedar Fort, Inc., www.cedarfort.com

Library of Congress Cataloging-in-Publication Data

McGaw, Elizabeth.
  Paleo on a budget : saving money, eating healthy / Elizabeth McGaw.
    pages cm
  Includes index.
  ISBN 978-1-4621-1327-9
  1. High-protein diet--Recipes. 2. Reducing diets--Recipes. 3. Low budget cooking. 4. Prehistoric peoples--Nutrition. I. Title.
  RM237.86.M3777 2013
  613.2'82--dc23
                        2013033523

Cover and page design by Erica Dixon
Cover design © 2013 by Lyle Mortimer
Edited by Casey J. Winters

Printed in the United States of America

10 9 8 7 6 5 4 3 2

TO DAD:

Thank you for inspiring me and giving
me the courage to learn how to cook.

CONTENTS

PREFACE

Hey there—my name's Liz. I'm short, I talk a lot, I blog, I love coffee, long walks on the beach, and high heels {did I mention coffee yet?}. And oh yes, I'm paleo. But I'm not only paleo; I'm paleo on a super-tight budget. I bet I got your attention with that last line, or maybe it was the long-walks-on-the-beach part?

Why am I paleo? Because being paleo absolutely rocks. Trust me on one thing—I don't do anything unless it's amazing, fun, and fabulous. Luckily for me, paleo hits on all three topics! But let's get into the nitty gritty, shall we?

Way back when {I'm talking maybe three years ago} I was wicked overweight, unhappy, and sick all the time. And by sick I mean I had serious digestion issues, I had icky skin, I couldn't really eat without getting sick, I was depressed, and I couldn't climb two flights of stairs without being out of breath. I was so desperate to lose weight and feel better that I was taking diet pills and Slim•Fast at the same time. Guess what? It wasn't working. After Mr. Not-So-Paleo {my husband} and I photographed a wedding, I saw a picture he took of me, and I literally cried. I had no idea I had gotten so bad and so big. It's not like I wasn't trying, either. Heck, I was even working out!

What was a girl to do? Well lucky for me I had a super awesome then-fiancé-now-husband who pointed out paleo to me. At first I thought he was joking. I mean, give up grains and eat meat? I thought that was the opposite of what I should be doing. Well, because of the point I was at with myself, I said, "Okay, what do I have to lose?" Answer: nothing.

I packed everything non-paleo up and stored it in the second bedroom, bought Robb Wolf's book *The Paleo Solution*, and went grocery shopping. Needless to say, the two hundred dollars I dropped for less than a week's worth of groceries floored me. But I was determined.

Fast forward a month or two and I was seeing results. I wasn't in severe pain after every meal, my skin was clearing up, and I was happy. Let me repeat that—I was happy. What wasn't too happy? My wallet. In fact, it was crying and begging me to stop. So I looked high and low for help on this whole budgeting thing and found there wasn't much out there for those of us on a tight budget looking to eat healthy foods. Thus my blog, *Paleo on a Budget*, was born. It's become my baby since then. I'm completely smitten with my blog and the people who read it. I love reading the comments, helping people, and seeing people thrive in a lifestyle that looks a little scary when they first give it a go.

Now you're probably thinking, *Okay, that makes sense why she loves paleo so much, but what about cooking?* Let's start off with this: I love to cook. Maybe I should repeat that. I *love* to cook! I've been cooking for as long as I can remember. My earliest {and best} memories are cooking with my dad. He's a chef by trade and has pretty much taught me everything I know.

I was the girl who could properly julienne before I could do long division. My dad and I used to also watch cooking shows together every Saturday on PBS, where I discovered different chefs such as Jacques Pépin, Julia Child, and many more. They gave me the inspiration to build a large repertoire of recipes and to push what was my "comfort zone." My love of cooking has only increased since then and is still growing. Loving to cook is and was a bonus when I went paleo because I was able to become a little extra creative with my recipes—so we didn't get overly bored eating the same thing day in and day out. {Hey, stir-fries are cheap!}.

And this all leads me here, to this book. This book is for my budget-conscious, penny-pinching, "I only have a dollar to my name" friends. Here's your resource {finally} for budget-friendly, filling, and yummy meals. Your kids are going to like these meals. Your spouses will like them. Even the not-so-paleos in your life will like them.

So enjoy this book, and you know how to find me if you have questions or need help. {That's right—I'm talking about online!}

PALEO 101
ACCORDING TO LIZ

While this is a paleo book and it focuses on the paleo diet, I want to make one thing clear from the start of our adventure together, and that's my take on paleo. In my mind, this paleo movement isn't about eating exactly as your great-times-a-zillion-grandparents ate. It's about creating a set of dietary guidelines that fit you and help your body function optimally—while still making you happy {and staying within budget}. What do I mean by that? Some people can handle dairy, but some can't. Some people like to add rice because they like the extra carbs, but some people can't handle a ton of carbs in any form because their bodies react one way or another. This doesn't make either version right or wrong. Your diet should be perfect for you. Are you going to have to adjust your diet as your body changes? Of course. I've been paleo for over two years now, and I'm still tweaking my diet to whatever I need at the time, whether I want to add muscle, maintain my weight, or lean out more. I make it about me and for me all the time.

So where does paleo come in in the grand scheme of things? Paleo gives you the confidence, tools, and guidance to strip back everything crappy you have ever eaten, and it gives your body a reset and the care that it really deserves. So when you see people "debunking" the paleo diet or saying that it's stupid or saying we need less meat or using whatever argument will be the latest one by the time this book is in your hands—don't listen. These people are coming from the standpoint that this diet and lifestyle is black and white based on

whatever guidelines they've found. In fact, there are different versions of the "guidelines" to fit different kinds of people and their different needs.

Make this diet personal from day one. Make this work for your body and your lifestyle. I know you're on a budget—you're reading this book, aren't you? So don't be ashamed to shop at the cheapest grocery store around if that's what you can afford. Rock it out and be proud of yourself for making a change.

And for the love of my morning coffee {and I LOVE my morning coffee} keep the crap out of your diet after you've put the work into being so awesomely healthy.

So now that I've given you my version of paleo, how about I give you a little bit more background information?

Where did paleo start? Most will argue it started in the Stone Age with your ancient ancestors, who were hunters and gatherers. Their diet mainly consisted of a high-fat and high-protein intake with some carbohydrates in the mix. It wasn't until the agricultural revolution that we started adding things like grains and more gluten into our daily diet. From there we became fairly dependent on foods like bread because it was an inexpensive way to feed people. Fast forward to 1975 when our friend Dr. Walter L. Voegtlin wrote the book *The Stone Age Diet*. Some would argue {and I'd agree} that this was the big push and start to the modern-day paleo movement. Why do I say modern? Because if you rewind a little, different points within history have documented cases of doctors and societies encouraging people to eat a diet that is made up of mainly good fats and proteins with a low amount of carbohydrates. {If you'd like more information on this side of things, I'd strongly suggest reading Gary Taubes's books *Good Calories, Bad Calories* and *Why We Get Fat.*}

Since Dr. Voegtlin's book, researchers such as Dr. Loren Cordain {author of *The Paleo Diet*} and Robb Wolf {author of *The Paleo Solution*} have hit the scene and have started to push paleo to where it is today.

Pretty cool history, right? I mean, come on—we get to eat how our ancestors ate, and we get to eat bacon. I'm not joking. You can eat bacon and even add other kinds of meat in the same meal if you want to!

Paleo is really easy. I think the hardest part of being paleo is taking those first few steps. I won't lie—it's a little weird at first. You're literally relearning how to eat and how to look at food. Just remember: if you have a particular health issue {such as leaky gut, autoimmune disease, and so on} you might need to follow a slightly different protocol as to what you can and cannot eat. Diane Sanfilippo, author of *Practical Paleo*, is a great person to check out because both her book and her website {www.balancedbites.com} offer a lot of information for different protocols!

Now it's probably time for some guidelines on the dos and don'ts. On the following pages is what I've come to understand and trust as the basics of paleo.

Now onto the super fun stuff!

THE DO EAT, DON'T EAT, AND MAYBE EAT LIST

PLEASE EAT LOTS OF:

meats • poultry • eggs • fish • vegetables • fruits and nuts

PLEASE DON'T EAT:

grains • legumes • peanuts • soy • corn • artificial sugars/sweeteners

most vegetable oils • gluten • overly processed foods • wheat

YOU CAN MAYBE EAT IF YOUR BODY SAYS IT'S OKAY:

dairy • white rice • raw honey/maple syrup • chocolate/paleo sweets • white potato

Let's start with your **do eat list**. He's a nice list, isn't he? He's pretty, he'll keep you full, he'll keep you healthy, and he'll help you achieve any athletic or weight-loss goals you might have. I like him . . . I like him a lot. Now when I say meat, you can eat pretty much any lean cut of meat you'd like. A lot of paleos will encourage you to eat organ meat and more uncommon meats if you can. I say do it if you can afford it. If you can't afford it or the thought of eating tongue or liver grosses you out, simply stick to the basics for now. As you get more comfortable with paleo, you can try new meats and expand on your repertoire.

Why do I want you sticking to these foods? Most of them are either high in fat or high in protein. Both will keep you fuller longer and help your body to function as efficiently as it possibly can while helping you achieve your goals. A lot of times the question is how much to eat of every-thing. I can't give you a set number of how much to eat because it varies from person to person, depending on what they're looking to achieve.

My rule of thumb is to make sure you're eating enough to feel full but not to the point where you're over-full all the time, and only, let me repeat, *only* eat when you're hungry. {And make sure you're hungry and not thirsty. A lot of times we become dehydrated and mistake that feeling as being hungry!} If you're not hungry for break-fast, skip it. It's your body saying, "I'm good. We're cool. We can eat later." Listening to your body and eating only when you're hungry isn't an easy thing to do. So be mindful of what your body wants and go from there!

Now if you're looking to lose weight, you might want to consider keeping fruit to a minimum or eliminating it from your diet until you've reached your goals. I find {and others do as well} that fruit and its sugars can keep the weight on and stall your progress. Not to mention, especially for me personally, fruit causes sugar cravings, which then causes carb cravings, which then causes me to have a paleo carb binge, and for me, that's never a good thing!

---

ext up is the **don't eat list**. This list is simple: no grains, wheat, soy, legumes, overly processed foods, and crap. Let me repeat: don't eat anything icky. You know exactly what I mean by *icky*—those donuts or that hidden bag of chips have got to go. Just put the book down right now and chuck those items in the bin. You'll feel so much better once you do!

The list of reasons to stay away from these foods literally goes on and on. A quick, simple explanation: grains/glutens/corn are generally a complex carb, which boils down to that one piece of pasta or that one bite of a bagel turning into sugar when it's digested. Your body is then going to treat it like glucose or fructose and store it as such. Which, for most of us, means it's going to become fat in our body. {Not the good kind of dietary fat—that icky kind of fat that can become visible on your body. You know what I'm talking about!} Legumes, which includes soy, can be difficult for your body to process, they contain what are considered *antinutrients*, and they can lead to immune system issues. This can then lead to leaky gut problems, which opens up a whole bag of berries you'll wish you hadn't. Most of these foods also have other common factors that are pretty crazy, and pretty scary if I'm being honest. But if I went on about those, we'd need a whole separate book to explain it all. So instead, at the end of this section, I'll list a few resources to check out that can explain it all in epic detail!

Now here's the extra kicker—be careful to read your nutrition label or ingredient lists for the foods you buy. You don't want to do all this hard work and have it thwarted by evil random ingredients. You'd be surprised by what you find in sausage, bacon, canned tomatoes, and so on. The first few times you grocery shop paleo-style, checking the labels is going to be a pain in your butt, I know. But it's worth it: once you study your favorite foods and their ingredients, and find out what you can and can't eat brand-wise, you'll be able to shop much more efficiently {which will save you time and money}.

Now the ultra-controversial **maybe eat list**. This list is only for people who know that their bodies can handle these foods. How can you find out? Let your body eat squeaky-clean paleo for at least thirty days. After those thirty days, add in, let's say, cheese or yogurt. Your body reacts well after a few goes? Good. You're all set to continue on that road and try other "maybe eat" foods if you want to. Don't add all of them back in at once or you'll never know what food is causing what reaction!

Any dairy that you consume needs to be super-high quality. I love and prefer raw cheese, but at least purchase the highest quality you can afford and make sure it's full fat. No more skim milk for you or "light" yogurt. Full-fat, my friends. Full fat. It will keep you fuller longer and is just overall better for you. And I want you to be as healthy as you can possibly be!

Things like rice and white potato are always going to be hit or miss, and they're always going to create controversy. There isn't a way around it. From what I've gathered, the main reason to stay away from both is because of the complex carbs within them {same as gluten/grains}. However, white rice and white potato are both benign and for the most part won't hurt or help you either way {unless you're on a serious campaign to lose weight}. I personally like to always cook my rice in chicken stock; the rice will absorb all the yummy, healthy qualities {and flavor} of the stock, making it a bit better for me. And white potato is a rare thing for me, but it's a nice treat every now and again.

Wait, Liz. Stop! What about store-bought meats, and what about the not-so-paleos in our life?

I can't believe I've waited this long to mention all of that! Here it goes:

When it comes to the great store-bought-meat debate, I say it's whatever you can afford. Don't stress your wallet on the higher-priced meats. Are the higher-quality grass-fed meats better for you? Probably. There's science behind it that says yes. However, the Liz science says that you need to pay your bills and eat healthy at the same time. So if that means you can only afford the bulk-discount ground meat, that's what you can afford. I swear it's better than eating a bowl of pasta tonight, and you're still going to see results in whatever you're trying to achieve. Just eat what you can afford. If you can afford grass-fed meat this week, go for it. If you can't next week and you buy discount meat instead, I promise there won't be any paleo police at your door the next morning. And if there are, call me. I'll bail you out.

As for the not-so-paleos, don't force them to be paleo. The quickest way to get them to never be paleo and to not like paleo at all is to force it on them. Try to work with them. If certain foods are triggers for you, and you don't want them in the house but they do, work out a compromise. Let's say they love bagels, but for you, bagels are too big of a temptation and you don't want them in the house {so that you can avoid the binge to rival all other binges}. Come up with a solution. Maybe they can store them and eat them at work, or something along those lines. This lifestyle is going to have to be give and take, and that's fine!

For instance, in our house I make all paleo meals, and if Mr. Not-So-Paleo asks for a non-paleo item to go with it, I'll make it for him. It's his choice, and I respect that. {Doesn't mean I don't tease him about ruining my "perfect paleo grocery cart" at the supermarket!} But on the flip side, he has to keep his snacks out of the cabinets in the kitchen {he's created another designated spot for them}. That way, when I'm cooking I don't have to stare at his snacks and grumble about all the ingredients in his Oreos. See? We've compromised, and everyone is happy. Truth be told, after three-plus years of me being paleo, the man himself is almost completely paleo. I'm guessing in another year the worst thing floating around our house will be white rice and white potato, which in the grand scheme of things is pretty awesome!

•　•　•

That's really the basic 101 on paleo. Like I said, it's easy-peasy, and you can do this no problem. Just so you know, the paleo community is huge {and I mean *huge*}. You can find many amazing blogs out there. If you have questions or need help, don't hesitate to reach out to one or all of us. We're here because we've been where you've been, and we want to help make this as easy for you as possible. If, however, after reading all this and looking at some of those blogs you're looking for more of an in-depth explanation of the whys and the science behind paleo, I encourage you to check out Robb Wolf's book *The Paleo Solution*, Melissa and Dallas Hartwig's book *It Starts with Food*, and Mark Sisson's book *The Primal Blueprint*.

WHAT TO
STOCK UP ON

Can we talk for a moment about your cupboards, pantry, and general stock items? Do you have a mini stockpile of important foods? Can you make at least two to three meals out of just what's in your house right now, without going shopping?

I know, it sounds expensive to have that kind of supply on hand and be that prepared, but it's not and will actually save you money down the road. I can't stress this enough: when you're on a budget, you need a stockpile of the ingredients you use and the foods you eat regularly. Everyone has days or weeks where buying groceries is going to stretch your budget to its breaking point, and having a stockpile will eliminate that stress for you.

How do you create this stockpile, and what should you have on hand?

Creating a stockpile is actually really easy. Make a list of all your essential food items, and whenever those items are on sale, buy a few extra. So if I find meats on sale or frozen veggies on sale, I'll pick up a few extra. That way, when money's tight, I'm not paying full price for what I need. Life throws curveballs all the time, and they can seriously stink at times, but that doesn't mean you can't still eat healthily.

And please don't feel like you have to go out and create your entire stockpile of extra food right this minute. Build it up slowly, steadily, and as you can afford it! Getting a fairly good surplus of awesome foods in my freezer and pantry took me about three months once I figured out that stockpiling was the best way to save money.

I also can't stress enough how important it is to seriously stockpile the non-food basics. You're always going to need toilet paper, aluminum foil, paper towels, toothpaste, soap, and so on. Those items, because they're more mainstream, go on sale all the time, and you can often find coupons for them. To some it sounds crazy, but if you have a nice surplus of this stuff on hand {from getting it on sale}, you won't be paying full price for it in two weeks when you need it. Therefore, you will have more money to buy things like bacon and meat.

Below is a list of what I like to have on hand all the time.

- At least 2–3 bags of frozen mixed vegetables

- 3–4 lbs. of ground meat, divided up as 1–1½ lb. packages and stored in the freezer

- 3–4 {14-oz.} cans of diced tomatoes

- 1–2 {28-oz.} cans of crushed tomatoes

- Your favorite dried herbs and spices. I think it's vital to have

  rosemary, oregano, parsley, basil, Italian seasoning, garlic powder, chili powder, cumin, salt and pepper.

- Aluminum foil {I know it sounds weird, but it's one of my best friends}

I know that's a basic list, but I think it's a great set of things to have in your home at all times. I also have a bigger stock-up list to shop for {see next page}, which I use when, for whatever reason, I get oddly low on pretty much everything. I don't utilize this list too often, but it's there for when I {and now you} need it!

MY BIG STOCK-UP LIST

Meats

- ❑ Ground beef
- ❑ Ground pork
- ❑ Steak {your favorite cuts}
- ❑ Chicken {whatever is on sale}

- ❑ Sausages
- ❑ Whole chicken
- ❑ _____
- ❑ _____

Herbs & Spices

- ❑ Dried basil
- ❑ Garlic powder
- ❑ Italian seasoning
- ❑ Dried rosemary
- ❑ Dried parsley

- ❑ Cumin
- ❑ Oregano
- ❑ Chili powder
- ❑ _____
- ❑ _____

Frozen Foods

- ❑ Pepper strips
- ❑ Peppers and onions
- ❑ Broccoli
- ❑ Mixed vegetables

- ❑ Green beans
- ❑ _____
- ❑ _____
- ❑ _____

Fresh

- ❑ Eggs {1–2 dozen}
- ❑ Onions
- ❑ Carrots
- ❑ Mushrooms
- ❑ Tomatoes

- ❑ Lemons
- ❑ Cucumbers
- ❑ Sweet potatoes or butternut squash
- ❑ _____
- ❑ _____

Other

- ❑ Canned diced tomatoes
- ❑ Canned crushed tomatoes
- ❑ Extra-virgin olive oil
- ❑ Extra-light olive oil

- ❑ Coconut oil
- ❑ Mustard
- ❑ Raw nuts
- ❑ Apple cider vinegar

PREP WORK
AND ITS LOVELINESS

rep work: it sounds like a scary phrase, but I swear it's not scary at all. What is prep work exactly? It's sitting down and creating a strategy that best fits you and your schedule to give you more time being you and less time being stuck in the kitchen throughout the week. Your prep work can include anything from making food at the beginning of the week to last you the rest of the week, to simply washing and chopping veggies the night before.

Prepping also includes making a meal plan for the week and picking meals throughout the week that blend together. For example, making something that has tomato sauce one night and making extra of the sauce to use as a base for chili another night. This will cut out most of the steps for the chili recipe, cutting your recipe prep time in half.

Here's an example of prepping one day in the week so you can make meals throughout the week easily and efficiently.

13

On your prep day:

- Make chicken stock {see page 44}. This will provide you with chicken meat and stock for soup this week.

- Hard-boil some eggs for munching on as a snack, adding to a lunch, and making egg salad for dinner.

- Make a double batch of tomato sauce {see page 43}.

- Make mini meatballs {see page 51}. You can use them for two dinners and for lunch and snacks this week.

On your prep day, you've set yourself up for {at least} five to six meals. Now you can create a menu for the week that looks like this:

Sunday dinner	Chicken and Meatball Soup
Use the chicken stock, chicken, and mini meatballs.	
Monday dinner	Zucchini Noodles and Sauce with Mini Meatballs
Use the tomato sauce and add mini meatballs to the sauce.	
Tuesday dinner	Chicken Salad and Sweet Potato Rounds
Use the chicken.	
Wednesday dinner	Egg Salad
Use the pre-hard-boiled eggs.	

Thursday dinner	Oversized Meatballs, Sauce, and Green Beans
Use the extra tomato sauce.	
Friday dinner	Kale and Tomato-ish Soup
Use the rest of the chicken stock.	
Saturday dinner	Pork Tenderloin and Cauliflower Rice

So for one afternoon's worth of work, you've cut down on prep time dinner for almost every night of the week. If you have the time and the flexibility to roll this way, I'd suggest you give it a try. It allows you to plan and prep everything, making your life much easier throughout the week.

However, you could be one of my friends who can't actually prep for the week because your schedule is jam packed from start to finish. I totally understand, but don't worry—there's a solution for that! Every meal you make needs to play double duty. When you make chicken for chicken salad, make double the chicken. When you make mini meatloaf, make extra and have it for snacks throughout the week. Stock up on extra frozen veggies and have a few stir-fries.

Your weekly menu could look like this when utilizing your prep strategy:

Sunday dinner	Chicken Fajitas
Making extra chicken to use later on in the week. {Instead of adding your veggies halfway through cooking, just add them in once the chicken is cooked, allowing you to make double the amount!}	
Monday dinner	Kale and Tomato-ish Soup
Make extra for Wednesday night.	

Tuesday dinner	Creamy Chicken with Zucchini Noodles
Use the chicken from Sunday night.	
Wednesday dinner	Leftover Kale and Tomato-ish Soup
Thursday dinner	Cube Steak and Panzanella Salad
Make extra panzanella salad.	
Friday dinner	Summer Shrimp Salad
Use the extra panzanella salad as the cold component of this salad.	
Saturday dinner	Burgers and Roasted Cauliflower Salad

As you can see, even if you don't have time to prep everything on one day, by making extra you can still utilize everything you're making to flow from one day to another.

THE RECIPES

The recipes you'll find in this book are fun, easy, and fresh for you to make time and again. There's no set right or wrong way to eat or serve them. Have fun and cherry-pick recipes throughout the book to make amazing meals for any time of day and any occasion.

THE BASICS

The basics: how I love you and think you're beyond important. The recipes in this section are probably some of the most versatile and vital, especially when you're on a budget. You can take any of these recipes and build at least two or three other recipes off of them with either leftovers or simply varying up the ingredients slightly.

You'll find many sauces and dips in this section because, let's face it, you can eat a stir-fry as is only so many times before it gets boring. Sauces and dips are nice, easy, and inexpensive ways to spice up any meal. Enjoy!

essing is a must-have basic item. It not only works for salads, but it can also double as a marinade, can act as an enhancer for particular stir-fries, and can even help bring life back to a meal you might have overcooked. The best part is that most of the time you will have all the ingredients you'll need in your home! I bet you could make at least two different kinds of dressing right this minute.

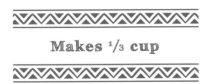

Makes ⅓ cup

DRESSING

1 tsp. mustard

1 part apple cider vinegar
{⅛ cup}

salt and pepper

½ tsp. rosemary

2 parts extra-virgin olive oil
{¼ cup}

How-to:

- Option A: Add all your ingredients to a mason jar or a container with a secure cover. Put the cover on and shake well. Do a quick taste for seasoning. When dressing is done, dress your salad and store the rest in the fridge.

- Option B: Add all your ingredients except extra-virgin olive oil in a bowl. Measure your olive oil and slowly whisk it into the bowl with the other ingredients. Do a quick taste for seasoning. When dressing is done, dress your salad and store the rest in the fridge.

AUTHOR'S NOTE:

Another dressing option is to thin out a batch of mayo {see page 21} with water or lemon juice, add in some flavorings {like garlic and herbs}, and you've got yourself a creamy dressing!

See the next page for some basic tips for good salad dressing.

Here are a few of the basics for a good salad dressing:

I like to use lemon juice, apple cider vinegar, or balsamic vinegar for one part of my dressing and then a good olive oil for the other part of it. Then I'll add in my favorite herbs, salt, and pepper to enhance the flavor.

You could add in some mustard or honey depending on the vibe you're going for with the meal. How much you use depends on your preference. Start with a teaspoon and add more if you need it.

The ratio of lemon juice/vinegar to olive oil depends on your preference. I like things quite tangy, so I generally do one part vinegar/lemon juice to two parts olive oil. If you don't like a lot of tang, do one part lemon juice/vinegar to three or four parts olive oil.

Oh mayo, how I love you. Not only are you yummy, but you're also versatile. You can go from a condiment to a dressing to the base of a sauce and back again without breaking a sweat. He was the first big "paleo staple" I learned to make. And let me tell you, I've changed this recipe many times since my first batch to get it perfect. I wanted to make sure anyone could use whatever mayo recipe I personally used, which is why this recipe doesn't call for a blender or mixer. Just a whisk and a bowl. If you have a blender and want to use that, by all means go on and use it!

Serves: Depends on egg yolk size and how thin or thick you like it

1 large egg, just the yolk

extra-light olive oil*

about 1 tsp. lemon juice or apple cider vinegar

salt and pepper

I can't give you an exact measurement for how much olive oil to use—every egg yolk, kitchen, person, pouring speed, phase of the moon, and so on make this an "as much as you need" situation. I will say you'll go through at least ½ cup of olive oil.

MAYO

How-to:

- In a small bowl, crack your egg and gently scoop out the yolk with your hand. This ensures you're only getting egg yolk into the mayo and not too much, if any, egg white.

- Place the egg yolk into a separate bowl. Give it a good whisk to break it up. Then slowly—let me repeat—*slowly* {so slowly it hurts} add in some olive oil while whisking. Don't add olive oil without whisking. It's crucial to make sure the emulsion takes almost instantly. {After you've become a mayo pro, you'll be able to tell almost instantly if your emulsion took!} Occasionally, I'll take a break from adding in olive oil and simply give it a really good whisk to ensure it's all nice and happy.

- You'll know it's all done when the majority of your mayo is a ball on your whisk {you'll be able to pick up your whisk and hold it upright and your mayo will stay put}.

- At this point, pat yourself on the back. You've made mayo!

- Now here comes the flavoring part. Add in a teaspoon or so of lemon juice or apple cider vinegar. Me personally? I like adding in lemon juice, but apple cider vinegar is cheaper. Go with whatever you have on hand right now.

- Mix that in, add in a little salt and pepper, and stir. Taste test and add extra of whatever is needed.

I'm half Greek, and I've got an awesome Greek family. They cook a lot. Because of this, I've had a lot of different foods over the years. One of my favorites is tzatziki. Tzatziki is traditionally a cooling Greek yogurt sauce that works well for anything spicy or heavy. This is my personal spin on it, without the yogurt and without the work. Also, the flavors in this version aren't traditional at all, but if you want to go traditional, by all means add in some fresh {or dried} dill and leave out the other spices.

Serves 2+ people

COOLING CUCUMBER SAUCE

1 batch of mayo
{see p. 21}

¾ cucumber

½ tsp. dried oregano

½ tsp. dried parsley

salt and pepper

¼ lemon juice

How-to:

◉ Make your mayo and then peel and dice {medium-fine} your cucumber.

◉ Add the cucumber into the mayo along with your other ingredients. Stir well and taste test for seasoning. Adjust as needed.

◉ *Boom!* Done. Enjoy!

AUTHOR'S NOTE:

This might sound weird, but this works with chili! Chili is spicy, while this sauce is cool and crunchy, making them the prefect match! This sauce also works with burgers, chicken, and so on and so forth.

Tartar sauce works with fish every time, and it doesn't really matter what kind of fish it is—baked, broiled, fried, and so on. Tartar sauce is an awesome, cool, and refreshing sauce that ties all the flavors together. However, I'm not a fan of traditional tartar sauce. It's normally gloppy and thick, and it tastes generic. This version is lighter, and it's going to be cheaper in the long run because you can make it on demand instead of buying it and letting half of it go bad in your fridge!

Serves 2–3 people

NONTRADITIONAL TARTAR SAUCE

1 batch of mayo
{see p. 21}

2 Tbsp. finely diced cucumber

⅓ tsp. apple cider vinegar

lemon juice to taste
{a few teaspoons}

1 tsp. mustard
{I like yellow mustard}

salt and pepper

How-to:

◎ Make your mayo and, using the same bowl, combine all the other ingredients with it.

◎ Mix everything well.

◎ Taste test for seasoning and adjust if needed.

◎ Serve and enjoy!

AUTHOR'S NOTE:

This should last a few days in the fridge. So if you're going to serve it at a party or get-together, you can make this ahead of time! Also, this is a thinner tartar sauce than you might be used to. If you prefer a thick tartar sauce, simply eliminate the lemon juice or the apple cider vinegar!

C aramelized onions are kind of like candy in the world of vegetables. They're beautifully sweet, and they're an amazing enhancer to almost anything. I love these with eggs, steak, chicken, other vegetables, and so on. The nice thing is you can make a large batch at the start of the week, store them in the fridge, and use when needed!

CARAMELIZED ONIONS

Makes: Depends on size of onion

1 Tbsp. fat of choice
{coconut oil, ghee, or grass-fed butter}

1 large onion, chopped in half and thinly sliced

salt

How-to:

- Heat a large skillet on medium-low with a good tablespoon of your favorite fat {coconut oil, ghee, or grass-fed butter}.

- Add in your thinly sliced onion and a sprinkling of salt. Stir and leave it alone for a little while, only stirring occasionally. Remember, low and slow wins this race. These are going to take a while, at least 15–20 minutes, to properly caramelize {instead of burning}.

- If you notice the pan starting to get dry, add in a little bit more of your fat of choice.

- You'll know the onions are done when they're a beautiful golden-brown color and when they're soft and sweet.

- Serve right away or store in the fridge. Enjoy!

oasted garlic is amazing—I know I say that about a lot of things, but I swear it's true! My dad and Mr. Not-So-Paleo both love roasted garlic, and they'll eat right out of the garlic bulb as is with a fork. As my dad says, "It's like butter." The best part is that this is so easy to make, and, as a bonus, it makes your home smell amazing.

Makes 1 garlic bulb

ROASTED GARLIC

1 bulb of garlic

olive oil

herbs
{optional}

How-to:

- Preheat your oven to 400°F.

- Cut the top off the garlic bulb, about an eighth to a quarter of the way down.

- Place the garlic on a medium-size piece of aluminum foil. Then drizzle a little bit of olive oil on it and rub it over the top. If you like, at this point you can sprinkle a little bit of your favorite herb on top.

- Bring up the sides of the aluminum foil and cover the bulb tightly.

- Place on a baking sheet and roast for at least 30–40 minutes, or until caramelized. The best way to tell if it's done is to squeeze the sides of the garlic {while in the foil}. If you can squeeze it easily, then it's done. {When squeezing, make sure you use a dish towel or something when touching the sides so you don't burn yourself!}

- When the bulb is done, allow to cool, remove from foil, and eat up!

I love fresh salsa. It's a fun, fresh thing to add to pretty much anything you want. It works on eggs, burgers, cauliflower rice, pork, chili, and the list goes on forever. I don't think this is a very traditional salsa recipe, but it works for me, and it's inexpensive to make! The key to a good salsa is good tomatoes. When picking your tomatoes out, smell them—make sure they smell fresh and like tomatoes. And give them a gentle squeeze. If they're too hard or too soft, they aren't ripe and they aren't the ones for you. And remember, you can adjust this recipe to be as traditional {or untraditional} as you like!

Serves 1–4 people

FRESH SALSA

3 medium tomatoes, finely diced

½ medium onion, finely diced

½ large cucumber, finely diced

juice of 1 lemon

juice of ½ lime

1 tsp. cumin

½ tsp. garlic powder or 1 clove of garlic, finely minced

½ jalapeño, finely diced

salt and pepper

How-to:

◉ Add all of your ingredients to a medium mixing bowl.

◉ Mix well, taste for seasoning, and adjust if needed.

◉ Enjoy!

uacamole is one of those yummy foods that becomes addictive fast. Lucky for you, I've got a super cheap way to make it. Now this guacamole isn't traditional {really . . . what in this book is?}. It's just yummy. If you want to add more traditional ingredients, feel free to do so. But I find fresh cilantro and other traditional ingredients to be kind of expensive for only one dish.

Serves 1–2 people

GUACAMOLE

1 ripe avocado

¼ small onion, finely diced

juice from ¼ of a lime

splash of lemon juice

½ tsp. ground cumin

¼ tsp. garlic powder

salt and pepper

How-to:

◎ Cut your avocado in half lengthwise and remove the pit. Scoop your avocado into a small mixing bowl. Then use a fork to mash it up. {You could of course toss it into a blender or food processor if you want it to be super smooth. But I prefer a chunkier, textured guacamole.}

◎ Add in the rest of your ingredients, mix well, and taste. Adjust seasoning if needed.

◎ *Boom!* It's done. Enjoy!

AUTHOR'S NOTE:

When it's exposed to the air, avocado will start to brown. To avoid this, I cover it with plastic wrap when I store it in the fridge, pushing the plastic wrap to the top of the guacamole {so they're touching}. This should help to keep it a pretty green color for longer.

C an I be honest? I've always hated applesauce. I used to think that every applesauce tasted like the stuff you get out of the little plastic cups from the grocery store—and that's not my idea of a good time at all. But last fall we went apple picking a few too many times {if there is such a thing} and had an overabundance of apples floating around. I decide to give homemade applesauce a try. And let's just say, I loved it! I swear I danced around the kitchen and couldn't stop eating it. It's delightful and foolproof. Not to mention, applesauce freezes like a champ. So you can make a ton come apple-picking season and freeze it to have year-round!

Serves 2–3 people

APPLESAUCE

apples

{A small to medium batch of applesauce takes about 4 apples. I like to use McIntosh, Cortland, and some other local apples.}

How-to:

- Preheat your oven to 350°F.

- Peel your apples.

- If you have an apple corer, use that to core the apples. Otherwise, use the Liz Method: split your apple into quarters and use a knife to cut out the core/seeds.

- Slice each quarter of apple. I like to slice them in half or fourths, depending on the size of my apple. Just make sure all of your pieces are evenly cut.

- Add all the apple pieces into a baking dish with high sides.

- Bake for 30–45 minutes, until your apples are soft and puffed up.

- Pull out of oven and stir/mash the apples with a fork. I like my applesauce a little chunky, so I don't go to town with the mashing, but if you want it super smooth, use a masher or even a food processor.

- Transfer applesauce to a container and store it in your fridge or freezer.

W hat can I say about zucchini noodles? They're one of my favorites because they're an inexpensive filler to any meal and a fun way for you and your kids to eat vegetables. Why is it in the basics section? Because you can use it any day, with almost any meal, and serve it hot or cold. Knowing how to make it is a great tool to have in your budget-friendly arsenal.

Serves 1-2 people

1 zucchini

ZUCCHINI NOODLES

How-to:

@ Wash and chop the ends off your zucchini

@ Use a peeler to peel the top green layer off your zucchini and discard.

@ Use your peeler again to peel the "noodles." I like to peel a side, turn the zucchini to a new side, peel again, and continue. This is to ensure you're using the zucchini evenly and getting the most noodles out of it.

@ Once you hit the core and can see the seeds, stop. But wait, don't toss the core! Save it in the freezer and add it into your next batch of vegetable or chicken stock {see page 44}.

@ Either store your noodles in the fridge or serve them.

@ Enjoy!

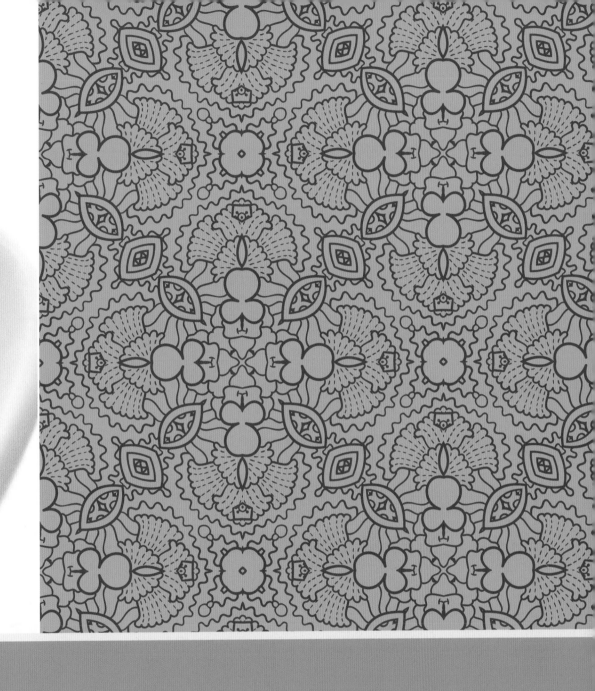

THE ESSENTIALS

This dish is hands down the biggest lifesaver when rocking paleo on a budget—heck, when you're rocking any type of eating on a budget. You can use any kind of meat and any kind of veggies and any amount of each you'd like. I suggest making extra because this will rock the next morning with some eggs or just as is. For veggies, I like to buy the frozen mixed bags when they go on sale. Most grocery stores will have them at around one dollar for one bag when on sale, and I stock up on them then and use them in my stir-fries. I try to stick to this rule of thumb for stir-fries: about one pound of meat, one large bag of veggies, and whatever my favorite flavorings of the moment are {herbs, chili powder, cumin, and so on}. Depending on the veggies, sometimes I'll add in a can of diced tomatoes or even some spinach. Below is just one of the many versions of a stir-fry that's common for dinner at my house! Want more ideas? Make sure to check out my blog!

Serves 2 people

STIR-FRY

fat of choice
{ghee, coconut oil,
or butter}

1 medium onion,
roughly diced

¾ lb. ground beef

1½ cups frozen spinach

1 {14-oz.} can diced
tomatoes, drained

salt and pepper

2 tsp. basil

How-to:

- Heat a large skillet on medium-high heat with your fat of choice. Toss your roughly diced onion in the pan.

- After the onion has softened for a few minutes, add your ground beef. Let it cook until it's halfway done and then add your spinach, diced tomatoes, salt and pepper, and basil.

- Let it finish cooking. Taste test and adjust seasoning if need.

- *Boom!* All done. Enjoy!

There really isn't anything more versatile than a tomato sauce. You can eat it as is, use it as a base for a chili, or use it as a condiment, and it's yummy any time of day. Not to mention, it makes the paleos and not-so-paleos in your life happy no matter how you serve it up. This also freezes really well. So make extra and save yourself some work down the road!

Serves 2–4 people

TOMATO SAUCE

1 Tbsp. grass-fed butter, ghee, or coconut oil

1 large onion, finely diced

3 medium carrots, medium to finely diced

2 celery stalks, finely diced

1 lb. ground beef

½ tsp. garlic powder or 1 clove of fresh garlic, finely minced

1 Tbsp. basil

1 Tbsp. Italian seasoning

3 Tbsp. apple cider vinegar

salt and pepper

1 {28-oz.} can crushed tomatoes

1 {14-oz.} can diced tomatoes

How-to:

- Heat a large pot on medium-high with a tablespoon of grass-fed butter, ghee, or coconut oil.

- Add your onion, carrots, and celery into the pot and stir. Let the veggies cook for about 5 minutes, stirring occasionally. They will start to soften.

- Add in your ground beef, garlic, basil, and Italian seasoning. Stir again and let your ground beef start to cook.

- When it's about halfway cooked, add in your apple cider vinegar, salt and pepper, and tomato products.

- Partially cover the pot and let it simmer on low for as long as you'd like, at least 45 minutes. About 10 minutes before serving, I like to pull the top off and let it continue to simmer. This helps the sauce to thicken up a little without adding any additional ingredients.

- Before serving, taste test your sauce and adjust seasoning if needed.

- Enjoy!

Seriously, who doesn't a love a good hot cup of chicken stock? It always perks up my mood and is a great thing to have in the freezer when you start feeling sick. {Chicken stock has the same properties as NyQuil minus all the icky ingredients!} The best thing is that when you make stock this way, you also get the chicken meat. So you're essentially getting a whole bunch of meals for very little money.

Did I mention this method is fast? Putting it together and on the stove takes me maybe 5 minutes, and draining and separating the chicken and chicken stock takes me maybe 10 minutes. So about 15 minutes of work results in yummy homemade chicken stock and chicken meat!

Makes 8–10 cups of broth and 5–6 cups of cooked chicken

CHICKEN STOCK

1 {4- to 5-lb.} whole chicken

2 medium onions

3 carrots

3 stalks of celery

a pinch of parsley

a pinch of oregano

salt and pepper

a splash of apple cider vinegar

11–12 cups water

How-to:

⊚ Rinse off your chicken and put it in a big soup pot. {Take out giblets/neck if included, unless you want to add it into the stock.}

⊚ This is where it gets easy. Just chop your onions in quarters—no need to peel—and add it in. Cut the carrots in thirds and rinse the celery and add them in {again, no peeling needed at all}.

⊚ Add in a big pinch of both parsley and oregano {about 1 tablespoon each} and then add your salt, a fair amount of pepper, and a good splash of apple cider vinegar {roughly 1 tablespoon}. Don't skimp on your salt. If you do, the stock will end up tasting a little off. You want to add at least a tablespoon of salt. After you make your first batch, you'll know how you'd like to adjust it if you need to.

⊚ Top with your water. Your water should come up about an inch above your chicken. Turn your stove on high heat. Bring your stock to a boil, then reduce your heat to low and simmer for 3–3½ hours, uncovered. If it starts to get low on liquid, top with some more water.

- When the chicken is done, pull it out and place it in a large bowl. Get a separate large bowl and a strainer and strain the stock into the bowl. Set aside.

- Shred all the chicken meat with your fingers {or two forks} and put into a separate bowl and store in the fridge or use for your meal. Throw out your remaining used veggies. You can either throw out the chicken carcass or save for making bone broth.

- When stock is room temperature, cover and put in fridge or use immediately for a soup {or just drink a mug of it}.

- Enjoy!

AUTHOR'S NOTE:

If you can't afford a whole chicken or if you can't find one, you can use large pieces of chicken with the bone in. Just make sure you get 4–5 pounds of it!

W ho doesn't love a roasted chicken? It's an all-in-one-pan meal. {Yay! Fewer dishes!} It's yummy and inexpensive to make. You should make extra of this dinner and enjoy the leftovers in various ways throughout the week. Looking for some ideas? Turn the leftover chicken into chicken salad {see page 143} or chicken soup {page 79}.

Serves 3–4 people

ROASTED CHICKEN

1 {about 5-lb.} whole chicken

2 onions

5 carrots

2 sweet potatoes

1 Tbsp. olive oil

1 tsp. rosemary, plus more

salt and pepper

¼ lemon

How-to:

◉ Preheat your oven to 350°F.

◉ Rinse your chicken under cool water and pat it dry. Place it in a roasting pan.

◉ Cut the top off of your onions {leaving the root intact} and then slice it in half. Remove the onion paper and slice each half into thirds, making sure to leave a little bit of the root attached to each section to hold it together while roasting. Place into a large mixing bowl.

◉ Peel your carrots and chop them into either thirds or quarters, depending on how large they are. Add those into the mixing bowl.

◉ Wash and cut the ends off of your sweet potatoes. Chop them into quarters. Chop each quarter into big wedges {I end up cutting them into quarters or thirds depending on the thickness of the sweet potato}. Add them to the bowl.

◉ Drizzle a tablespoon or so of olive oil into the bowl and sprinkle in a teaspoon of rosemary, followed by salt and pepper. Use your hands to mix everything together.

@ Sprinkle some salt, pepper, and rosemary into the cavity of the chicken. Then cut your quarter lemon into two pieces and place those inside the chicken cavity as well.

@ Put a teaspoon of olive oil into your hand and rub it onto the outside of the chicken and then sprinkle it with salt, pepper, and rosemary {you can be as generous as you like here}.

@ Place all of the veggies around the chicken in the roasting pan. Roast the chicken for 1½–2 hours, until the juices run clear between the leg and thigh when you cut there and the chicken reaches 165°F at the thickest part with an instant-read thermometer.

@ Remove the chicken from the pan and place on serving platter or a cutting board and place veggies on a serving platter. Cover both with aluminum foil and let sit for 15 minutes.

@ Once your 15 minutes are up, carve your chicken and serve it with the veggies.

@ Enjoy!

P ot Roast is probably one of the most well-known classic dishes, next to chicken soup of course {see page 79}. I tried to make this version as cheap and as easy as humanly possible, and I think I succeeded! This doesn't require any browning or any touching of the stove. So really, it's not only easy but also foolproof. You're welcome! And as always, make extra. The leftovers rock, and the veggies are great the next morning with some eggs! Not to mention, this method creates a fair amount of liquid that you can save and use as a base of a beef stock later! So really, a pot roast can give you a fair amount of meals without having to do that much work!

Serves 2–4 people

POT ROAST

2 medium onions, medium-diced

3 large carrots, diced into bite-size pieces

1 medium sweet potato or butternut squash, diced into bite-size pieces

1 {8-oz.} container button mushrooms; de-stemmed, cleaned, and cut into quarters

1 tsp. basil, divided

1 tsp. parsley, divided

salt and pepper

1 {2-lb.} chuck roast

¾ cup water or beef stock

grass-fed butter, ghee, or olive oil

How-to:

◎ Get your slow cooker set up on your counter in a safe, easy-to-access spot.

◎ Add your onions, carrots, sweet potato, and mushrooms to the bottom of the slow cooker.

◎ Add ½ teaspoon of basil, ½ teaspoon of parsley, and a sprinkle of salt and pepper to the veggies. Use your hands to mix it a little.

◎ Place your roast on top of your veggies and sprinkle remaining basil and parsley along with a little bit more salt and pepper.

◎ Gently pour your water or beef stock on top. Then either dot the roast with some butter or ghee, or drizzle a little bit of olive oil on top of the meat. This rounds out the flavors nicely!

Directions continue on next page.

- Set slow cooker on low for 6–8 hours or on high for 4–6 hours. Honestly, it's a pot roast. . . . It'll be ready when you're ready, so if you go over the prescribed timing, don't stress—it's going to be totally fine.

- Serve and enjoy!

AUTHOR'S NOTE:

The sweet potatoes do come out a little soft and almost mashed like, but I really like that; it provides a nice contrast to the beef and carrots. If you don't like that texture to your potatoes, either completely leave them out or add them in about halfway through the cooking process {you can do this by simply lifting up the beef, adding the potatoes, and then placing the meat back on top}.

Also, I know most pot roasts call for garlic, but I personally don't like garlic in a pot roast {fresh or dried}. If you're a fan of garlic, you can either add in 2 finely chopped garlic cloves when you add the veggies, or you can cut a few cloves in half {or thirds} and stud it into the meat. Either way will make for a yummy pot roast.

These things are not just addictive, but they're also cheap to make. I mean really cheap. You only need a pound of ground beef to make a boatload of these little beauties. My favorite part? You can have them on hand to pop in your mouth when you're hungry, you can serve them as an appetizer at a party, or you can make a bunch and then freeze and save them for tomato sauces and soups throughout the next few weeks. This could even be a fun thing to pack the kids for their school lunches!

Makes 64 mini meatballs

1 lb. ground beef

1 small onion, finely diced

1 small carrot, finely diced

1 button mushroom

1 large egg

¼ tsp. garlic powder

½ tsp. ground cumin

1 tsp. rosemary

1 tsp. basil

salt and pepper

MINI MEATBALLS

How-to:

- Preheat your oven to 350°F.

- Now you have two options to start:

  - Option A: Combine all of your ingredients into a large mixing bowl as they are.

  - Option B: Sauté your onion, carrot, and mushroom in some ghee, coconut oil, or butter before adding them and the rest of your ingredients into the mixing bowl.

    {Remember either way to crack your egg first into a separate smaller bowl, just in case you've got yourself a bad egg, and then add it into the larger bowl with everything else.}

  - The difference between these options? Option A will give you a slightly crunchy carrot and onion, whereas option B which will have everything softer in texture. I myself am a fan of option A, mainly because I'm just that lazy.

Directions continue on page 53.

@ Now here's where it gets messy. Get your hands right in there and mix it up. And by mix, I mean really mix it. Make sure everything is combined well, but at the same the same time don't overmix your meat {delicate balance, I know}. Overmixed meat will produce a tough meatball, and you and I would both like to avoid that I'm guessing.

@ All nice and mixed? Awesome! Now line a large baking sheet {or even two smaller ones} with aluminum foil.

@ Use a measuring teaspoon and scoop some meat out onto the palm of your hand. Roll it into a ball, place it onto the sheet, and repeat. The meatballs don't need to be spread too far out from each other on the pan, but make sure they're not touching!

@ Bake for 15–20 minutes or until cooked through.

AUTHOR'S NOTE:

The mushroom in this is completely optional, I just like the bit of added flavor to the meatball. Feel free to add in some finely diced pepper or really any sort of veggie that makes you happy, or leave it out all together! Same thing with the seasoning—if you don't like basil or rosemary, swap it for your favorites!

R oasted veggies are yummy. They're an easy side dish to make and can be used in a variety of main dishes. Almost any veggie can be roasted, but my favorites are carrots, onions, broccoli, cauliflower, peppers, sweet potatoes, and squash. Be aware: if you roast different veggies at the same time, make sure to watch them because some veggies will roast faster than others! This recipe is a basic 101 on vegetable roasting. I'm going to talk about onions and carrots, but apply this method to any vegetable, adjusting cooking time as needed!

Serves 2–3 people

ROASTED VEGGIES

3 carrots

2 onions

olive oil

salt and pepper

herb{s} of choice
{optional}

How-to:

◉ Preheat your oven to 375°F.

◉ Peel your carrots and then chop them first in half, then lengthwise in half. If you wish, you can chop them again into quarters or thirds. Place them onto your baking tray.

◉ Cut your onion in half lengthwise {so each side has part of the root} and peel the onion paper off. Then cut the onion in half lengthwise again, leaving part of the root attached to each piece. You want to make sure you have root on each piece because it'll keep the onion layers intact as it roasts! If you need to, depending on the size of your onion, you can cut the quarters in half.

◉ Place the onions on the pan as well. Drizzle some olive oil on top and sprinkle on some salt, pepper, and herbs if you're using them. Toss the carrots and onions together gently with your hands and spread into a single layer.

◉ Roast for at least 30 minutes, until everything is soft and roasted, flipping them halfway through cooking.

◉ Enjoy!

EVERYDAY MEALS

These recipes are just that: perfect for any time, any day. They're affordable, fun everyday recipes for you to enjoy. I completely admit that about 99 percent of the time I'm lazy or I just don't have time to cook like I'd like to, and I'm guessing I'm not the only one. This is why most of these recipes don't take a long time to prep and are quick and easy to make—but they are certainly not short on flavor. The few that are somewhat lengthy in prep and cooking, like shepherd's pie and zucchini lasagna, are great for Sunday night dinners or special occasions!

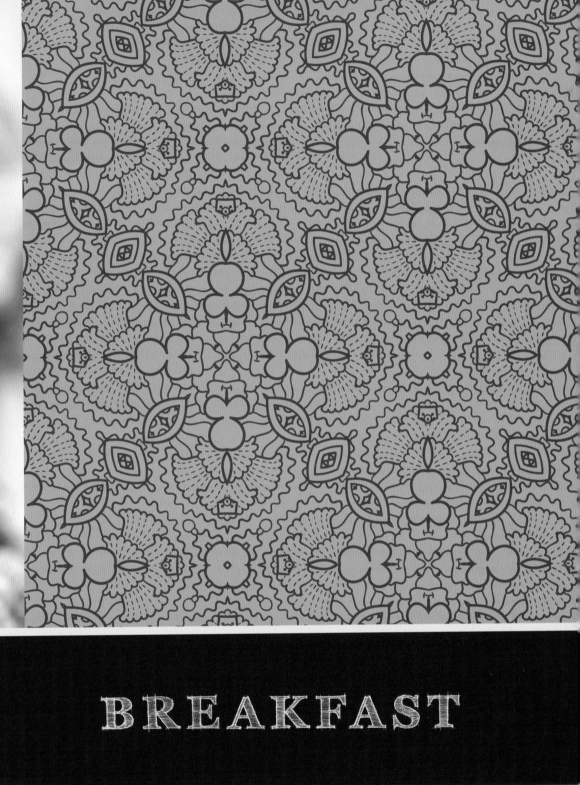

BREAKFAST

Every now and again I like a breakfast patty or sausages with my eggs {even for dinner}. It's an easy breakfast item to make, and this recipe makes a ton of them. This way you can preportion for your week in advance, freeze them, and then pull them out of the freezer at the start of the week and *boom!* Easy, hearty, healthy breakfasts!

Makes 20–25 patties

BREAKFAST PATTIES

1½ lbs. ground pork

¼–½ tsp. ground cinnamon

1 tsp. basil

1 tsp. oregano

salt and pepper

fat of choice
{ghee, coconut oil, or butter}

How-to:

@ Combine your pork, cinnamon, basil, oregano, and salt and pepper in a mixing bowl and mix well. {If you're a huge cinnamon fan, add half a teaspoon; if you're just a casual cinnamon fan like me, add in a quarter teaspoon.}

@ Heat a large skillet on medium-high with a little bit of your fat of choice.

@ Once the meat mixture is all mixed together and your pan is hot, make a mini patty, around the size of a quarter. Fry it on both sides, cook through, and taste test for flavor. This way you can decide if it needs more flavorings or if it's ready to go. Adjust flavorings as needed.

@ Then make small breakfast-sized patties and begin to fry them {you might need to make these in batches}.

@ Transfer patties to a plate to cool slightly. Then either store or serve.

@ Enjoy!

I'm a big fan of being lazy in the morning when it comes to my breakfast. Let's face it: between the family, trying to get ready, and the million other things on the to-do list, remembering to eat {never mind cook} breakfast doesn't seem to rank quite as high as it probably should. So to make up for this fun little habit of mine, I've had to come up with an easy solution, which ended up being egg muffins. I make a dozen or so at the beginning of the week, stick them in the fridge, and eat them throughout the week.

The best things about these little beauties? They're not only yummy, but they also make great snacks after a workout {or any time of day, really}. And you can freeze them! What's better than that, right? You could have an egg muffin party one day—make a bunch and freeze them. Then you'll be set for weeks—with only a few hours' worth of work!

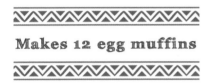

Makes 12 egg muffins

1 {3-oz.} sausage, casing removed and crumbled/cut

1 small onion, finely diced

salt, pepper, and your favorite herbs/spices

8 large eggs

¼ {8-oz.} container mushrooms; cleaned, de-stemmed, and diced into bite-size pieces

EGG MUFFINS

How-to:

◎ Preheat your oven to 350°F.

◎ In a large bowl, add your sausage; onion; and salt, pepper, and dried herbs to taste. I normally use about 2 teaspoons of dried basil and half a teaspoon of ground cumin in mine! But use whatever you like or have on hand!

{If your sausage is in small enough pieces, you won't have to precook it. If you're nervous about that, panfry the sausage pieces quickly on the stove for 2–3 minutes prior to adding it into the egg mixture.}

◎ Add your eggs into the bowl—I crack one into a smaller bowl first, then I add it into the big bowl, just to make sure the eggs aren't bad!

Directions continue on next page.

- Mix everything together really well. Then add in your diced mushrooms, and mix again.

- Grab your muffin tin {I use a 12-muffin nonstick tin, but if yours isn't nonstick, make sure to liberally grease it with butter or ghee!}

- Scoop the mixture evenly into the muffin tin. You can fill these pretty close to the top.

- Pop your tin into your oven, cook for 20–25 minutes, until the eggs are cooked through and your "muffins" are a light golden-brown color on top.

AUTHOR'S NOTE:

Play around with the filling and use what's on hand! Don't go out and buy ingredients special for these. If you have leftover hamburger, use that, or use leftover stir-fry from last night! Just make it cheap and affordable for yourself.

I've had a lot of people ask me for eggless breakfast ideas. And truth be told, I'm not a breakfast kind of girl. I eat leftovers for breakfast frequently, or I eat egg muffins {see page 63}, or I just skip breakfast altogether. {And trust me, it's not a bad thing like we were all taught as kids. If your body doesn't want breakfast, don't force it—remember, eat when you're hungry.} But this recipe makes me want breakfast. Not just any breakfast, but a Sunday morning breakfast. I love those breakfasts.

Serves 2–3 people

EGGLESS BREAKFAST SCRAMBLE

3–4 slices of bacon
{and a few extra for yourself}

1 small sweet potato

1 medium onion

2 sausages, chopped
{breakfast link–sized}

1¼ cups chopped
frozen broccoli

½ tsp. parsley

salt and pepper

fresh lemon juice

about ½ Tbsp. ghee
or butter

½ {10.5-oz.} container
cherry tomatoes, cut in half

How-to:

◉ Heat a large dry skillet on medium heat and add your slices of bacon. Now you'll notice the recipe requires 3–4 slices, but I recommend making at least 2 slices for yourself to eat while cooking. More if you have kids, spouses, and pets roaming around the kitchen looking for some!

◉ While the bacon is cooking, wash and finely dice your sweet potato and set aside. When the bacon is done cooking, remove it from the pan and let it sit on a plate off to the side. But don't remove the bacon fat, that's what you're cooking everything else in!

◉ Add in your sweet potatoes and let them start to cook. The idea here is that because they're so finely diced, you don't have to worry about them taking forever to cook. Just make sure after you stir them into your bacon fat that you let them sit there for a few minutes to cook and crisp up on one side.

◉ Stir again, let sit, and repeat.

Directions continue on page 67.

◎ Now while the sweet potatoes are super happy in the bacon fat, finely dice your onions and add those into the pan. Stir and let them sit again for a few minutes.

◎ When your sweet potatoes are almost completely cooked, add in your sausage and broccoli and stir again. Let it continue to cook.

◎ Once you're at the almost-done phase, add in your parsley, salt and pepper, a squeeze of fresh lemon juice, and ghee or grass fed butter.

◎ When it's all done, turn the heat off and taste test for seasoning and adjust if needed. Then add in your cherry tomatoes, give it a quick mix, and serve!

AUTHOR'S NOTE:

If you don't have bacon and sausage on hand, don't stress! I think any combination of pork and chicken {even turkey} would work well with this breakfast. But I don't think red meat would go over too well with the other flavors.

hy *rustic*? When Mr. Not-So-Paleo and I ate this, the first thing we thought of was *rustic*. Not weird rustic, just awesomely country-rustic inspired. It's a super easy breakfast, and it's filling. I'm also of the frame of mind that this would be one stellar dinner!

Serves 2 people

RUSTIC BREAKFAST

butter or ghee

1 small onion

1 {3-oz.} sausage link

4 large eggs

1½ cups frozen spinach

½ Tbsp. basil
{or your favorite herb}

salt and pepper

1 tsp. fresh lemon juice

How-to:

@ In a skillet, get some butter or ghee melting on medium to medium-high heat while you dice up your onion. Add your onions into the pan and let them start to soften.

@ Pull the casing off your sausage and crumble it into the pan and let it cook.

@ While that's cooking, heat up a second smaller skillet with some butter or ghee and fry up your eggs {I like to cook two at a time}.

@ When your sausage is halfway cooked, add in your spinach, basil, salt and pepper, and lemon juice. Let it finish cooking.

@ Divide your filling onto two plates, top with two eggs each, and enjoy!

The original idea behind this recipe was more of a burger-egg-sandwich. But it ended up being great as just a flat, almost pizza-like dish. I wanted to mix the hot and cool textures in multiple ways with this breakfast item, and I think I hit the mark. It's a fun meal that I think kids and adults are both going to like! The nice thing is, is that this recipe makes a lot of burgers, so you can either serve at least six people if each person gets one, or you can serve a few people and have leftovers for lunch or dinner!

Serves 1–6 people

butter, ghee, or coconut oil

THE BURGER:

¾ lb. ground beef
{or pork}

¼ tsp. garlic powder

½ tsp. cumin

¼ tsp. oregano

1½ tsp. chili powder

salt and pepper

THE REST:

1 fried egg per serving

cooling cucumber sauce
{see page 23}

½ onion, thinly sliced

hot sauce
{optional}

BURGER-EGG YUMMINESS

How-to:

@ Heat a large skillet with a little bit of fat on medium-high heat. Combine all your burger ingredients into a bowl and mix it all together.

@ Form your burgers and add them to the hot pan as you go. You can make them any size you like, but I like to make them somewhere between the size of a slider and an actual burger. Cook your burgers to your desired level of doneness, making sure to flip them halfway through cooking.

@ Once the burgers are done, transfer them to a plate and cover it with some foil to keep them warm. Turn skillet down to medium heat.

@ Crack your egg into the skillet and fry it up to your liking. Place your egg on a plate, top it with some cooling cucumber sauce, a few slices of onion, and then your burger. If you'd like, drizzle on some hot sauce and spread it across the top of your burger for an extra kick! Repeat for all burgers.

@ Serve and enjoy!

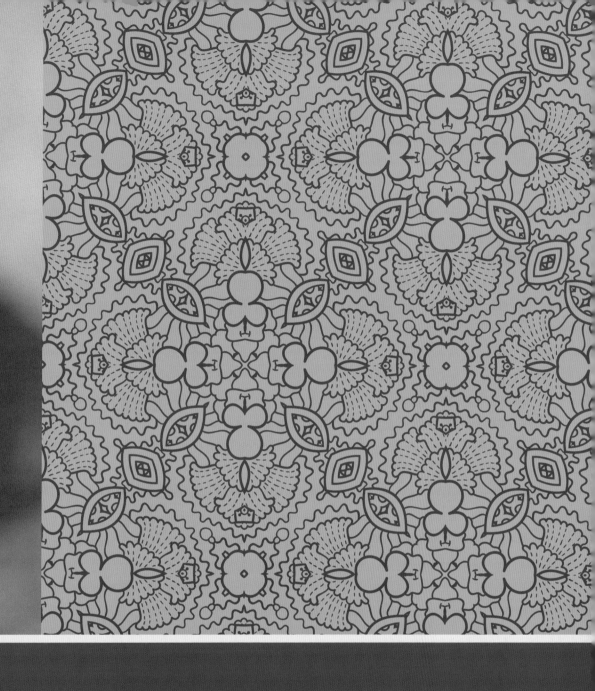

SOUPS + SALADS

So this soup is super easy to make, but what soup isn't easy? It's my take on "chicken and dumplings" even though I've never actually had chicken and dumplings. Still, this is what I imagine it should and would taste like! You know, all filled with meat and veggies, and just yummy. You can easily make this soup ahead of time and freeze it to have on hand. Make extra because soup for breakfast is a great way to start your day!

CHICKEN AND MEATBALL SOUP

Serves 3–4 people

butter, coconut oil, or ghee

1 medium onion

3 medium carrots

2 stalks of celery

1 lb. ground beef

cracked pepper

a pinch of salt

3 tsp. Italian seasoning, divided

3 cups shredded or diced cooked chicken

8 cups chicken stock

salt and pepper

How-to:

- Heat a soup pot on the stove on medium heat with about a tablespoon of butter, coconut oil, or ghee. While it's heating, medium dice your onion, carrots, and celery.

- Add them into the pot and let them start to soften. While that's happening, put your pound of ground beef into a bowl, add in some cracked pepper and a pinch of salt along with one teaspoon of Italian seasoning. Mix everything together well.

- Take your ground beef and make bite-size meatballs {2 teaspoons' worth of meat per meatball}. I like to form a meatball and drop it into the pot and continue on until all the meat has been used up.

- Give the soup a little bit of a stir, being careful not to break the meatballs.

- Add in your chicken, chicken stock, remaining Italian seasoning, and salt and pepper to taste.

- Cover and let simmer on low for at least an hour.

- Enjoy!

AUTHOR'S NOTE:

If you have mini meatballs already made {see page 51}, you can use those instead!
Use half a batch's worth of meatballs and add it in at the same time you add in
the chicken and chicken stock.

SLOW COOKER DIRECTIONS:

Place all ingredients into slow cooker and let cook on low for 6–8 hours or on
high for 4–5 hours.

This soup is epic and is a huge favorite on my blog. I've heard that it is kid, husband, and non-paleo approved, which in my book is some of the highest praise you can get. And we really should just take a moment to thank Mum for the inspiration for this recipe. She makes a stellar soup from which I've based this recipe. So thanks, Mumma! Oh, and here's the skinny on kale: if you don't have any or its too pricey to get, just switch it out for spinach, cabbage, or some other leafy green. Just buy what's on sale and fits your budget—it'll all be yummy.

Serves 2–4 people

KALE AND TOMATO-ISH SOUP

butter, ghee, or coconut oil

1 medium onion,
medium-diced

1 big bunch of kale or
1 {10-oz.} box frozen Kale

1 lb. spicy sausage

1 {12-oz.} bag frozen
pepper strips
{or 2 fresh peppers, sliced}

1 {14-oz.} can diced
tomatoes

⅓ {28-oz.} can
crushed tomato

½ tsp. garlic powder
{or 1 clove garlic, minced finely}

1 Tbsp. oregano

½ Tbsp. Italian seasoning

½ Tbsp. basil

4 cups chicken stock
{see p. 44}

fresh lemon juice

salt and pepper

How-to:

◉ Heat a soup pot with butter, ghee, or coconut oil and add the onions. Let them become friends for around 5 minutes.

◉ While that's softening, if you're using fresh kale, start to separate the leaves from the stem, tear up into pieces, and put them into a large bowl.

◉ Take the casing off of your sausage, crumble it into the pot, and let it start to cook.

◉ Add in your peppers and kale. If using fresh kale, add it all in and then cover your pot. It'll steam the leaves, which will make them more manageable. If using frozen kale, just add it straight in give it a stir after a few minutes to start to break it up.

Directions continue on next page.

- Add in the rest of your ingredients and stir.

- Cover your pot and let it simmer on low for a minimum of 30 minutes.

- Right before serving, squeeze in half a lemon's worth of juice. Stir and taste test for seasoning and adjust as needed!

AUTHOR'S NOTE:

When I serves this, I like to finish it off with a smidge bit more pepper, another spritz of lemon juice, and a drizzle of good-quality extra-virgin olive oil!

hicken soup is the bee's knees in the world of soup. It's yummy, it's easy, and it's a classic. Like a classic movie, if you will. Yes, that's exactly it. This is a classic movie—it's a black-and-white, beautifully done, and fabulous-anytime sort of movie.

Serves 2–4 people

CHICKEN SOUP

about 1 Tbsp. butter, ghee, or coconut oil

1 medium onion, medium-diced

3 carrots, medium-diced

2 stalks of celery, medium-diced

¼ medium butternut squash

4 cups shredded or diced cooked chicken

8 cups chicken stock
{see p. 44}

1 Tbsp. parsley
{fresh or dried}

salt and pepper

juice from ½ lemon, plus more
{optional}

How-to:

- In a big soup pot on medium heat, add butter, ghee, or coconut oil. Then add in your onions, carrots, and celery. Let them start to soften.

- While those are going, peel and medium dice your butternut squash. Drop that into the pot, stir, and let it soften a little.

- Add in your chicken, chicken stock, parsley, and salt and pepper {to taste}. I also like to add half a lemon's worth of juice. This is optional, but it brightens up the flavors really nicely. {If you don't have lemon on hand, you can absolutely add apple cider vinegar instead!}

- With the lid propped a little, simmer the pot on low for at least an hour or until the butternut squash is cooked all the way through.

- When serving this soup, I like it in a mug {a comfy-cozy feeling} with another spritz of lemon juice.

- Enjoy!

It's no secret that I absolutely adore chili. Why do I adore chili so much? It's easy to make, it's a one-pot meal {hello, lack of extra dishes}, and I can use whatever I have on hand in it. Which means I don't buy anything extra special for this chili. Remember, every single chili recipe you find is nothing more than a method. It can be tweaked and edited depending on what you have at home. If you have leftover steak, chicken, pork chops, sausage, veggies, or whatever, add it in. {You can also make it in a slow cooker.} Chili is a great way to make a big dinner without having to buy a lot and to get all the extra food out of your fridge before it goes bad.

Serves: 2–4 people

CHILI

coconut oil, ghee, or butter

1 medium onion, medium-diced

2 carrots, medium-diced

2 {3-oz.} spicy sausages

1¼ lbs. ground beef

1 medium sweet potato, diced; or ¼ butternut squash, diced

salt and pepper

4–5 Tbsp. chili powder

2 Tbsp. cumin

1 Tbsp. each of dried basil, dried oregano, and Italian seasoning

1 tsp. garlic powder

½ tsp. red hot pepper flakes

2 Tbsp. apple cider vinegar

1 {14-oz.} can diced tomatoes

1 {28-oz.} can crushed tomatoes

How-to:

⊚ Heat a very large pot on medium with coconut oil, ghee, or butter. Once it's melted, add your onions and carrots and let them start to soften.

⊚ Remove the casing from your sausage and crumble it into the pot. Add in your ground beef and diced sweet potatoes and give everything a big stir.

⊚ Add in all of your spices and apple cider vinegar and give it all another big stir. Let it cook for a few minutes to let everything become friends.

@ Then add in your diced tomatoes and crushed tomatoes, stir again, and partially cover and let simmer on low for at least an hour. The general rule of thumb with chili is the longer it sits, the better it tastes.

@ Enjoy!

AUTHOR'S NOTE:

I like to top my chili with avocado, guacamole, salsa, chopped cashews or almonds, or shredded cheese. I also strongly encourage you to make extra. Chili freezes well and can provide you with a quick meal one night in the not-so-distant future. It is also a great filling to use in egg muffins {see page 63}.

This sweet potato salad is quick and easy. It's not meant to be fussy or fancy. Just a good old-fashioned "I need a quick side dish or just something to eat because I had a wicked rough WOD." This particular recipe was designed so you can take it and run with it {not literally—you might spill some}; add things like sausage, bacon, different fruits, nuts, and so on if you want to. Or you can eat it as is. That's what I do normally. Heck, when I make sweet potato salad, it doesn't even make it onto a plate—I simply eat it out of the mixing bowl.

SWEET POTATO SALAD

Serves 2–3 people

1 medium sweet potato

olive oil

salt and pepper

½ small onion

1 small stalk of celery

1 batch of mayo
{see page 21}

2 tsp. mustard

½ Tbsp. apple cider vinegar

1 tsp. dried basil
{or favorite herb}

How-to:

◎ Preheat your oven to 400°F.

◎ Wash and chop your sweet potato into bite-size pieces. Place them on a baking tray, drizzle with a little bit of olive oil, and sprinkle with salt and pepper. Toss it all together and spread into a single layer on the baking tray.

◎ Bake for 15–20 minutes, until cooked through and starting to get a wee bit crispy.

◎ While that's roasting, finely dice your veggies and make your mayo. A quick tip: make your mayo in a bigger mixing bowl than you normally would, so you can add everything into it and you won't have to wash an extra dish or waste any mayo!

◎ To your mayo bowl, add in your veggies, mustard, apple cider vinegar, and seasoning. Mix it together well.

◎ When your sweet potatoes are done, let them cool for a few minutes on the tray {and yes, I highly suggest snacking on a few of them right now}. Add them into your bowl. Mix everything well, taste for seasoning, and adjust if needed.

◎ You can either serve immediately or cover and store in the fridge until you're ready for it.

C an I be honest for a moment? I normally can't stand cauliflower. It for some reason freaks me out. I can do cauliflower rice on occasion, but other than that, I'm not its number-one fan. But this salad? I can't get enough of it! Which is crazy, I know. But this means that even the pickiest of eaters could potentially love this dish. Bonus round: you can use it as a main dish or as a side dish. I served this as is one night when we weren't overly hungry, and it was perfect. Be warned: you might have to hide it from family members until it's time to eat—I caught Mr. Not-So-Paleo "taste testing" the roasted cauliflower a few times.

Serves 2–4 people

ROASTED CAULIFLOWER SALAD

1 medium head
of cauliflower

olive oil

salt and pepper

coconut oil, ghee,
or butter

1 medium onion,
medium-fine diced

2 {3-oz.} sausages
{spicy sausages are best here}

½ tsp. basil

2 Tbsp. apple cider vinegar

1 large ripe tomato
{I like Hot House tomatoes here}

How-to:

- Preheat your oven to 400°F.

- Rinse your cauliflower, cut it in half, and cut out the core {using a good knife for this will make it easier}. Then proceed to cut your cauliflower into florets. I personally don't like to leave a lot of stem on the floret, but it's a personal choice. Also, keep the florets to a little bit under bite-size pieces. This way they cook faster and are easier to eat.

- Place the florets on a baking tray, drizzle a little bit of olive oil, and sprinkle with salt and pepper. Roast for 20–30 minutes, until they start to get a little color on them and are cooked through. Quick note: These won't crisp up like broccoli does, but nonetheless they still taste amazing!

- While your cauliflower is roasting, heat a medium-sized skillet on medium with coconut oil, ghee, or butter. Add your diced onion into the pan.

- Let your onion start to cook a little. Remove the casing from your sausages and crumble them into the pan and add in your basil. Stir and let it continue to cook until the sausage is fully cooked.

◉ Place your onion, sausage, and roasted cauliflower into a large bowl. Add in a sprinkle of salt and pepper and your apple cider vinegar. Mix well. Then chop your tomato into bite-size pieces, add it to the bowl, and give it one more mix.

◉ Enjoy!

Steak salads are a staple in my house. Why? Because there are points throughout the week when you want something fresh to eat and easy to make, and that's where this beauty comes into play. The nice part is you don't have to actually make most of it the day you eat it. Let's say you make broken-down burritos {see page 166} tonight, make extra of the steak & onions and save it for tomorrow night when you make this steak salad. And you don't have to use steak if you don't like it or don't have any. Chicken and cut up pork works here if you don't have any steak on hand. And at the end of the day you are going to be one very happy camper you made this salad.

STEAK SALAD

Serves 2 people

½ butternut squash, roasted
{see p. 111}

coconut oil, butter, or ghee

1 medium onion, medium-diced

¾ lb. steak

salt and pepper

lettuce of choice

extra-virgin olive oil

fresh lemon juice

slivered almonds
{optional}

How-to:

- Roast the butternut squash {see page 111}.

- While the squash is roasting, heat a large skillet with coconut oil, butter, or ghee on medium heat. Add in your onions and let them start to soften. While that's happening, cut up your steak into bite-size pieces.

- Add your steak to the skillet and sprinkle it with salt and pepper. Let it cook to your preferred level of doneness.

- When your steak and butternut squash are done, add some lettuce to each plate. How much depends on your preference.

- Layer on butternut squash and then your steak and onions. How much of each once again depends on your preference and how hungry you are. Then top with a little more salt and pepper, drizzle with some extra-virgin olive oil, and spritz on some lemon juice.

- If you're so inclined, you can top the salad with some slivered almond for a crunch factor. Serve and enjoy!

AUTHOR'S NOTE:

This recipe generally makes us huge salads or we have leftovers. Save the leftovers for another salad tomorrow, use in a stir-fry, or even add them into a chili!

Egg salad is in my mind an underdog in the culinary world. Most people think he's boring and only meant for barbecues in the summer. Well I'm here to change that! Egg salad is yummy and fun to eat. My favorite thing is that it's both paleo and not-so-paleo friendly. So put this recipe on the must-try list and serve it up for lunch!

Serves 2 people

EGG SALAD

5 large hard-boiled eggs

1½ stalks of celery

1 small onion

1 batch of mayo
{see p. 21}

1 tsp. apple cider vinegar

1 tsp. yellow mustard

½ Tbsp. Italian seasoning

½ Tbsp. basil

salt and pepper

How-to:

@ Chop your eggs up into small pieces and put into a bowl. If you prefer a smoother egg salad, you could pulse them in your blender instead, but I like the actual bits of egg instead of a finer texture.

@ Finely dice your celery and onion and add them into the bowl.

@ Add in the rest of the ingredients and mix well.

@ *Boom!* It's done. Enjoy!

AUTHOR'S NOTE:

This egg salad works well with extra bits added in. If you have leftover hamburger, bacon, sausage, and so on, they'd taste great in here! If you do add extra bits, make sure to add a little bit more mayo to compensate.

This recipe is probably one of my all-time favorites to make in the summer. It's easy and doesn't require any cooking, which, when it's 95 degrees out, is a must in my book! It's based off of an Italian panzanella salad, which is generally made with day-old bread. Obviously we aren't adding any bread to this, so I've used the mushrooms instead to give the salad the same hearty feeling it would traditionally have. Also, the leftovers are fabulous. You can toss them into an omelet or scrambled eggs the next morning for something a bit different and fun! The veggies I have here are somewhat optional. If you have other vegetables on hand that are yummy raw, you can add those instead of or in addition to something. Make sure when picking out your ingredients that they're fresh and ripe. This salad is based on the vegetables, so they need to taste great to make this a stellar side dish instead of an average one!

Serves 2–4 people

½ a medium onion, finely chopped

1 large cucumber, chopped into bite-size pieces

2 large tomatoes, chopped into bite-size pieces

¾ {12-oz.} container mushrooms; cleaned, de-stemmed, and chopped

½ cup chopped fresh basil or 1–2 Tbsp. dried basil

¼ cut chopped rosemary or 1 Tbsp. dried rosemary

salt and pepper

olive oil

1 fresh lemon

PANZANELLA SALAD

How-to:

@ Add your washed and chopped veggies into a large mixing bowl along with your herbs.

@ Add in salt and pepper, a healthy drizzle of olive oil {at least two tablespoons}, and the juice of one lemon. Mix it up, taste, and adjust seasoning if needed.

@ Either serve immediately or place in fridge for later. Enjoy!

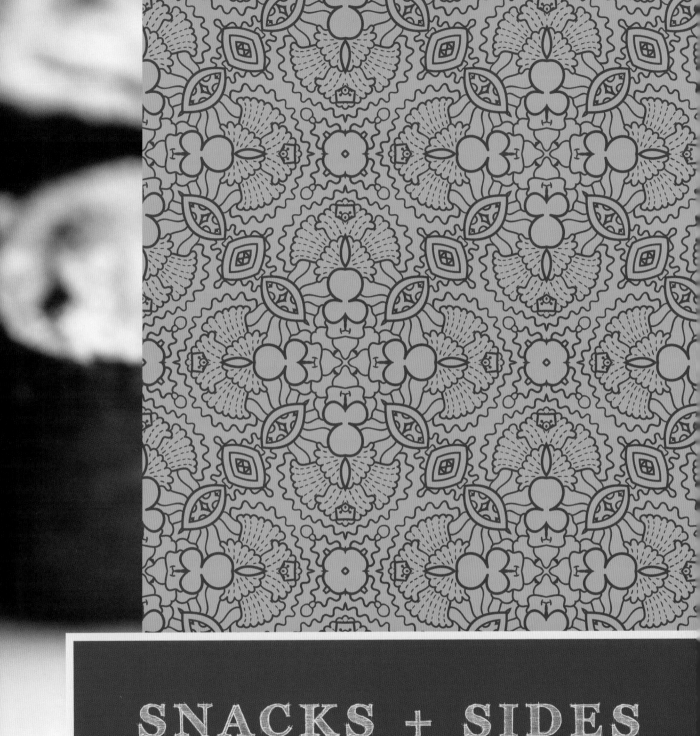

SNACKS + SIDES

I n my pre-paleo days, I had this amazing little breakfast/snack number called a "taco bagel," which consisted of a bagel, butter, salsa, and cheese. I can't lie—it was good. Mr. Not-So-Paleo still requests that I make him one around the holidays as a breakfast treat. But after last holiday season, I wanted to find a way to make a similar one for myself. Lo and behold, I give you the non-bagel-cheese-less-almost-a-taco bagel, or "Liz's Favorite Snack" for short. And I think this is actually better than the original recipe!

Makes 5–6 snacks

ghee or butter

paleo crackers, made larger
{see p. 102}

fresh salsa
{see p. 31}

LIZ'S FAVORITE SNACK

How-to:

◉ Take your ghee or butter out of the fridge to allow it to soften a little.

◉ Make some paleo crackers, but instead of the normal half-tablespoon size, use a tablespoon measurement, and, if needed, bake for an extra 1–2 minutes until golden brown on the edges.

◉ Once the crackers are done and cooled, put them on a serving plate and slather in ghee or butter. Then top with however much salsa you'd like {I'd suggest a few tablespoons.} If you don't overload it with salsa, you'll be able to pick it up and eat it as is. If you overload it with salsa, you might have to use a fork.

◉ Serve and enjoy!

AUTHOR'S NOTE:

If you eat dairy, you can absolutely add on some raw shredded cheese and then microwave it for a few seconds to melt it.

know, I know—ants on a log is the coolest thing ever! Now some of you are probably shaking your head at me, thinking, "Liz, really . . . you added this in?" Some of you haven't heard of ants on a log, and others are doing a happy dance because anything that involves the phrase "ants on a log" has got to be beyond epic! And well, not to toot my own horn, but these are *amazing*. Best part? These are super quick to make! They are the world's best after-school kids' snack, and the kids get to feel cool because they're eating a fun hands-on snack.

Serves 1–2 people

ANTS ON A LOG

1 cucumber

almond butter
{or your favorite nut butter}

raisins
{or your favorite dried fruit}

How-to:

@ Cut the ends off your cucumber, peel it, and chop it in half widthwise. Then cut it lengthwise down the center. From there, scoop out the seeds/guts until you're left with little tunnels.

@ Spread as much almond butter as you like inside the tunnels {I use a spoon for this} and top with raisins.

@ Enjoy!

T his is a recipe that my *yiayia* {grandmother} used to make me on a regular basis when I was over for dinner. I've always had a love of all things vinegar and tart, so of course this was one of my big-time favorites. Heck, Mr. Not-So-Paleo is pretty in love with these guys too. {Which begs the question, why didn't I make them for him sooner? Ha! I have no idea either.}

This very easy side dish can be made a few days in advance if need be. Not to mention, it's perfect for hot summer days because there's no cooking required and there are only three ingredients. I know, I know—it's amazing!

Serves 2–3 people

1 medium cucumber, peeled and cut into thin slices

balsamic vinegar

pepper

BALSAMIC CUCUMBERS

How-to:

- Add your cucumber slices to a gallon-sized ziplock bag and then add a few splashes of vinegar. I can't give you an exact amount because it depends on how vinegary you want this and how many slices of cucumber you have. My rule of thumb is to fill a quarter of the way up the cucumbers {or less}.

- Add in a little black pepper. Close the bag, making sure to get all the air out. Shake it around a little, evenly distributing the balsamic vinegar through the cucumbers.

- Let it lay flat in the fridge until you're ready to serve, or at least for 30 minutes.

- When ready to eat it, empty the contents into a bowl and serve!

AUTHOR'S NOTE:

Yiayia used to make this in a bowl instead of a ziplock bag, but I find that that method uses way more vinegar, which can become costly—good balsamic vinegar is pricey. But if you are only making a few slices, feel free to let them soak in a bowl. Just remember to cover them before putting them in the fridge.

good deviled egg is probably one of the easiest elegant things you can make for yourself. There are so many different versions of deviled eggs out there that I wanted to give you a basic one. This way, when you want to get crazy with them and add in bacon or crab meat, you have a fantastic base to work with. So go hard-boil yourself a bunch of eggs and make these.

Makes 10 deviled eggs

DEVILED EGGS

5 large hard-boiled eggs

3 Tbsp. mayo
{see p. 21}

2 tsp. yellow mustard

¼ tsp. paprika, plus more

salt and pepper

How-to:

@ Cut your hard-boiled eggs in half lengthwise, scoop the yolks out, and put the yolks into a small mixing bowl.

@ Use a fork to mash all of your yolks well. {If you want, you can pulse the yolks in a food processor, but I hate making extra dishes to wash later—so mashing with a fork it is for me!}

@ Add in your mayo, mustard, paprika, and salt and pepper. Mix well.

@ Scoop a little bit of filling back into each egg and then sprinkle a little bit more paprika over the top.

@ Enjoy!

AUTHOR'S NOTE:

If you wanted your deviled eggs to look pretty, use a pipping bag with a star tip to fill them up!

Pre-paleo, I was obsessed with cheese and crackers or crackers and butter. I was literally the girl who would have bread or crackers just to eat butter. So alas, I've had to come up with my own cracker-like recipe. These are a little chewy in the center, but the edges are crispy. They're like a lovely combination of a cracker, wafer, and soft cookie. Slather these with Kerrygold butter or ghee, and you will be one happy camper. These would also be good dipped like a chip with some salsa {see page 31} or guacamole {see page 32}. You might want to play around with how thick or thin you like them—try it a few ways before you settle on your favorite!

Makes 22 crackers

PALEO CRACKERS

1 cup almond flour

2 large eggs

2 Tbsp. melted butter

2 Tbsp. water

1 Tbsp. rosemary

½ tsp. garlic powder

¼ tsp. salt

a dash of pepper

How-to:

@ Preheat your oven to 375°F.

@ Combine all of your ingredients in a medium bowl and mix well. Remember to crack your eggs first in a separate bowl and then transfer to the real mixing bowl to avoid bad eggs and shells.

@ You can then do one of two things: Either line a cookie sheet with aluminum foil and oil it down just a little, or you can just use a nonstick cookie sheet. I find that the crackers get crispier on the nonstick cookie sheet {only by a little}, but whatever you have on hand will work.

@ Once you've got your cookie sheet ready to go, use a half tablespoon to scoop your mixture onto the cookie sheet. {If you don't have a half tablespoon, use 2 teaspoons per cracker.} Use a finger to gently push the mixture out a little so it becomes thinner and rounder. Repeat until you run out of batter.

@ Bake for 6–8 minutes, until your crackers are crispy on the outer edge and slightly soft in the middle.

AUTHOR'S NOTE:

I made these savory, but if you want them sweeter, swap the rosemary for cinnamon and add a teaspoon or so of raw melted honey.

Whoa. I know, right? Paleo non-fish sushi. I think this is a killer thing to make for the kids for lunch, to serve as an appetizer, or to have for dinner one night. You can of course make this with fish if you'd like, but you have to make sure, if it's raw, you're using sushi-quality fish {I can't stress enough how important this is}. You can also make this with different flavorings. Heck, have a sushi party one night! Think about it: a kids' sushi party. They can make their own {all you'll have to do is cut them up}, they eat healthy, you're not doing a ton of cooking, and everyone has a blast! For the nori sheets, check out the Asian section in your grocery store. It's generally on one of the bottom shelves and comes in a pack of large sheets {don't get the small sheets}.

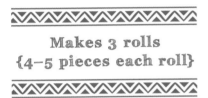

**Makes 3 rolls
{4–5 pieces each roll}**

PALEO SUSHI

¼–½ head of cauliflower

about ¼ lb. precooked shredded chicken

½ cucumber

3 sushi nori sheets

pepper

1 fresh lemon, cut in half

How-to:

◉ Make your cauliflower rice: cut ¼–½ a head of cauliflower into florets, add to a blender or food processor, and pulse until it looks like "rice." Move it into a microwaveable bowl, cover with plastic wrap, and microwave for 4–5 minutes.

◉ Shred up around ¼ of a pound's worth of chicken. You can dice it up and cook it, but make sure it's in small, thin pieces if you do. For this I generally use the shredded chicken I get from making chicken stock {see page 44}.

◉ Peel and thinly slice your cucumber into strips. I like to cut the seeds out to prevent the roll from getting watery.

◉ Now make sure you have a good size space around so your nori will lay flat. Run the nori under cool water for a few seconds, making sure it all dampens a little. {Don't have the water at full blast—a low-medium water pressure is good.} Lay the nori out on your surface.

◉ About ¼ inch down the nori, scoop 2–3 tablespoons of cauliflower rice onto it. Pat it out into a rectangle, leaving a little bit of room at each end. I normally make the rectangle about ½–1 inch wide. Lay 1–2 strips of cucumber in the center of your cauliflower rice. The cucumber doesn't need to overlap; you just want it to spread across the width of your rectangle.

Directions continue on next page.

- Do the same thing with your chicken. I normally use 2–3 thin pieces.

- Then give it a crack of pepper and a spritz of lemon juice.

- Here comes the fun part: roll it up! Roll it as tightly as you can, it might take you a few goes to get the hang of it, but once you do you'll be rolling these things at mach speed!

- Then use a sharp knife {it helps if you run the knife under hot water first} to cut off each end of the nori and then divide the roll into as many pieces as you'd like, I normally cut it into 4–5 pieces. Continue on until you have as many rolls as you need

- Serve and enjoy!

AUTHOR'S NOTE:

I normally serve this with a thinned-out mayo {see page 21} as the sauce!

S tuffed mushrooms are one of my favorite appetizers ever. They work for holidays, parties, family functions, and those nights you simply want to treat yourself to something special! Even better, if your kids will eat mushrooms, these make a great after-school snack that you could make the night before and reheat when they come home.

Makes as many mushrooms as are in your container

1 {12-oz.} container mushrooms
{I like to use the white button mushrooms}

1–2 small sausages
{breakfast link–sized}

2 large eggs

salt and pepper

2–3 sprigs of rosemary, finely chopped

STUFFED MUSHROOMS

How-to:

- Preheat your oven to 350°F.

- De-stem, wipe off, and place the mushrooms into a baking dish, mushrooms bowl side up, so to speak.

- Chop your sausages into tiny pieces and add them into a mixing bowl.

- Add your eggs, salt and pepper, and rosemary to the bowl. Mix well.

- Spoon filling into each mushroom cap. I like to fill them to the top, making sure each mushroom has sausage in it.

- Cover the baking dish tightly with aluminum foil and bake for at least 20 minutes. The time depends on the size of your mushrooms and amount of filling. They're done when the filling is set and the eggs are cooked.

- Be *very* careful when peeling back the foil to check if the mushrooms done—there is a lot of steam, and no one likes burnt fingers!

AUTHOR'S NOTE:

You can add in a sprinkling of a raw cheese to the f if you eat dairy!

oleslaw is one of my favorite summertime side dishes. It works with pretty much anything you cook on the grill and can be made in advance {like the night before} to make your get-togethers a breeze. You'll notice that this recipe has few ingredients and isn't complicated. I did that on purpose. You're on a budget, I'm on a budget, and there's nothing wrong with making you and your friends and family a yummy, simple coleslaw. Since this recipe will give you a great base to start with, you're more than welcome to amp it up with different-colored cabbages {like red cabbage, but he is awfully expensive}, different veggies, and so on.

Serves 2–4 people

1 batch of mayo
{see p. 21}

¼ medium head of cabbage

½ medium carrot

2 Tbsp. apple cider vinegar

salt and pepper

COLESLAW

How-to:

@ Make your mayo in the bowl you intend to make your coleslaw in {this saves dishes and doesn't waste mayo}.

@ Cut the core out of your quarter of cabbage. Cut your cabbage into very thin strips starting on the "open" side {the side where you can see the inside of the cabbage}. If you start to get bigger pieces because they're closer to the core, either leave them out {and save for soup} or slice them into thinner slices. You should end up with 2–3 cups of shredded cabbage when you're done. Add into the bowl with your mayo.

@ Use a vegetable peeler to make thin slices of the carrot {similar to how you make zucchini noodles; see page 37}. I like to do this right over the bowl. You can add as much or as little carrot as you like, but I add in ½–¾ of a cup.

@ Add in your apple cider vinegar and a sprinkling of salt and pepper. Mix it well. Taste test to see if it needs more pepper or vinegar and adjust if needed. Cover coleslaw and leave in the fridge. The longer it sits in the fridge, the less crunchy it gets. The general rule of thumb is to let it sit for at least 3 hours, and I wouldn't go past 1–2 days. It will get fairly soft by that point, and the leftovers won't be as yummy.

@ Enjoy!

Well if we have *B-sprouts* for brussels sprouts, we need *B-squash* for butternut squash, yes? Yes! Why am I giving roasted butternut squash its own recipe? Because it's one of those vegetables people don't think to chop into tiny cubes and roast. Therefore it needed a voice. More often than not, in the fall you can get butternut squash for a steal, making it cheaper than sweet potatoes and other yummy vegetables. You can literally swap this out for any of those without worry about compromising on flavor. The best part? These guys are normally pretty big, and if you're only cooking for two people, you can get away with only roasting a quarter to a half of one and saving the other quarter or half for soup, chili, mashing {see page 116}, and so on. You can also roast a fair amount ahead of time and use throughout the week in salads, breakfast, and stir-frys to make your life yummy and easier!

Serves 1–2 people

ROASTED B-SQUASH

1 medium butternut squash

olive oil

favorite herb
{optional}

salt and pepper

How-to:

- Preheat your oven to 375°F.

- Cut your butternut squash in half in the center {separating the bottom round end and the longer end}. Peel and cut one half in half and then proceed to cube into bite-size pieces.

- Add the butternut squash to a baking tray in a single layer.

- Drizzle with some olive oil, sprinkle with a good amount of your favorite herb if you'd like, and then lightly sprinkle with some salt and pepper. Use your hands to toss everything together and smooth it back into a single layer.

- Bake for 30–45 minutes or until browned and cooked through all the way. I generally like to go for slightly crispy when I'm roasting them because they get really light and airy inside and are wicked flavorful.

- Let them cool a little before serving—or you can be like me and burn your mouth while "taste testing" . . . several times!

- Enjoy!

These little cuties are addictive! They're an awesome mix of crunchy and fluffy, which might sound odd, but it makes for one yummy side dish. These guys are also pretty cool because you can easily make the first part of the recipe ahead of time and then finish baking them either later on that day or the next day to make your life easier!

Serves 4 people

SWEET POTATO ROUNDS

1 Tbsp. butter, ghee, or coconut oil

2 sweet potatoes

salt and pepper

rosemary

How-to:

- Preheat your oven to 375°F.

- Heat a large skillet on medium-high with at least a tablespoon of butter, ghee, or coconut oil. While it's heating up, cut your sweet potatoes into about ¼-inch-thick rounds.

- Drop some of your rounds into the skillet and let them brown. After a few minutes, flip them over and let them brown on the other side. I normally split the rounds into at least three batches since I don't want to overcrowd your pan.

- Once the rounds are browned on both sides, place them on a large baking sheet. Sprinkle the top side with salt and pepper and liberally with the rosemary.

- Pop them into the oven and bake for 15 minutes.

- Pull the rounds out of the oven and flip each one over on the baking sheet and then re-sprinkle with salt and pepper and rosemary.

- Bake for an additional 10 minutes.

- They're done. Enjoy!

I was never the kid who had to be told to eat her veggies; I loved them. But I never tried brussels sprouts {or *B-sprouts*, as I like to call 'em} until I went paleo. These yummy little things can be cooked to suit your tastes, and they're inexpensive when you buy them frozen, making them the perfect side dish! I love to serve this spicy B-sprout recipe with mustard and burgers!

Serves 2–3 people

B-SPROUTS

coconut oil, ghee, or butter

1 {6-oz.} bag frozen brussels sprouts

2–3 Tbsp. apple cider vinegar

1 tsp. red pepper flakes

salt and pepper

How-to:

@ Before cooking, I like to leave the brussels sprouts on the counter for about 15 minutes so they start to thaw a little.

@ Heat a skillet on the stove on medium-high with coconut oil, ghee, or butter. Then cut your brussels sprouts in half and add them to the pan to let them start to cook.

@ Once these start to get a little bit of color on them, add in the apple cider vinegar, red pepper flakes, and salt and pepper.

@ Taste test the brussels sprouts for seasoning and adjust if needed. When they're fully cooked and have some nice color on them, they're done.

@ Enjoy!

So this recipe is more of a method than an actual "this is the way you must make it" recipe. Well, when you really think about it, most recipes in this book are methods, which is what makes them so budget friendly! Anyway, you can use this method to make really anything that's hearty "mashed"—sweet potato, pumpkin, other kinds of squash, and so on. The big thing to remember is that this method makes a mashed squash with texture to it, so it's not the smooth and almost pureed in texture kind. If you prefer a very smooth consistency, you'll need to pop it into a blender or a mixer instead for the best results!

Serves 1–2 people

¼ butternut squash

¼ medium onion

1 Tbsp. butter, ghee, or coconut oil

1 tsp. rosemary
{or favorite herb}

salt and pepper

MASHED BUTTERNUT SQUASH

How-to:

@ Fill a pot with water and set on the stove. Don't turn it on just yet, though.

@ Peel and medium-dice your butternut squash. The smaller you dice it up, the quicker it will cook.

@ Peel and dice your onion {small to medium dices}. Add both the squash and onion into the pot of water.

@ Cover the pot, but tilt the lid so steam is able to escape. Set on medium-high to boil. {Here's a cool trick: if you're in a rush, set that stove on high and watch it like a hawk so it doesn't make a mess and bubble over—it should cook wicked quick. If you're not in a rush and in fact don't care how long it takes, you can set it on medium-low and do other things like wash dishes, make other food for the week, and so on.}

@ You'll know the squash is cooked when you can pierce it easily with a fork.

@ Carefully drain your squash and onions and leave them in the pot once drained. {Why make more dishes, right?}

@ Add in your butter, ghee, or coconut oil; rosemary; and salt and pepper. Mash the mixture. I use a fork to mash things up, but you can use a potato masher if you want to.

@ Taste test for seasoning, adjust if needed, and you're all set!

oesn't asparagus feel like one of those special side dishes? When I was a kid, it was a big deal if we had asparagus with dinner, and there was generally a mad rush to pile it on our plates. Why? Because asparagus is normally so expensive to feed more than two people! To save on costs, I've used frozen asparagus, allowing us to eat more and not break the bank! If you only love fresh asparagus, you can use it here—just be mindful that if you're going to be feeding a large number of people, this might not be the most budget-friendly side dish!

Serves 2–3 people

LEMON ASPARAGUS

½ Tbsp. ghee
or grass-fed butter

½ medium onion,
finely diced

1 {8-oz.} bag frozen
asparagus

juice from ¼–½ lemon

salt and pepper

How-to:

◉ Take your asparagus out of the freezer and leave it on the counter.

◉ Heat a medium-size skillet on medium-high with your ghee or grass-fed butter.

◉ Add in your onion and let it start to soften. Then chop your asparagus in half, add it to your skillet, and let it cook through.

◉ When the asparagus is almost done, add in your lemon juice and salt and pepper. Taste test a piece of asparagus and adjust seasoning if needed.

◉ Serve and enjoy!

AUTHOR'S NOTE:

This is also great with red pepper flakes added in for a kick! I'd use anywhere from a quarter to a half of a teaspoon at first and add more if you like it extra spicy!

M aking these made me feel like I was making the ultimate side dish. I mean, think of it: it's a sweet potato, baked twice . . . with sausage. Talk about crazy yummy! Not to mention, this dish is easy and kid friendly. What more could you ask for in a side dish?

Serves 2 people

1 medium sweet potato, baked

2 Tbsp. coconut oil, ghee, or butter, plus more

½ small onion, finely diced

1 {3-oz.} sausage

salt and pepper

1 Tbsp. coconut milk, almond milk, or full-fat milk, plus more

1 tsp. Italian seasoning
{or your favorite dried herb}

½ tsp. garlic powder

TWICE-BAKED SWEET POTATO

How-to:

- Preheat your oven to 350°F.

- Wash and scrub your sweet potato and then poke holes in it with a fork several times. Bake it for 45–60 minutes, until it's cooked all the way through.

- Once your potato is baked, set it aside and allow to cool.

- Heat a small skillet on medium-high with coconut oil, ghee, or butter.

- Add your onions to the skillet and let it start to soften. Remove the casing from your sausage and crumble it into the pan. Add in a dash of salt and sprinkle of pepper and allow to finish cooking.

- While your skillet of onions and sausage is cooking away, cut your sweet potato in half lengthwise.

- Scoop the inside of the sweet potato out into a small bowl and use a fork to mash it up a little bit. Make sure to save the skins because you'll be refilling them in a few minutes!

- Add your cooked onions and sausage into the small bowl. Also add in your 2 tablespoons of coconut oil, ghee, or butter; 1 tablespoon of coconut milk, almond milk, or full-fat milk; Italian seasoning; and garlic powder.

- Mix it all together well. Adjust with more fat of choice or milk of choice if you need to. Scoop half of the mixture into one half of the potato and the rest of the mixture into the other sweet potato half.

- Bake for 15 minutes and serve.

- Enjoy!

AUTHOR'S NOTE:

If you're a white potato eater, you can absolutely swap out the sweet potato for the white potato!

FISH

Nothing says budget quiet like a can of tuna, am I right? I remember way back when, when Mr. Not-So-Paleo and I were pretty poor—tuna was our best friend. Oddly enough, now that I've gone paleo, I've learned to eat even better for an equally-as-tight-budget, making tuna an "every now and then" recipe instead of a staple meal. Having said that, I now have way too many variations for tuna salad up my sleeve. This is a generalized recipe that will work as a quick budget-friendly meal or something to make in bigger quantities for a summer get-together with family. Please remember when purchasing your can of tuna to look at the ingredients and make sure they are only tuna and water or tuna and olive oil. You don't want six hundred other ingredients mixed in with it! And you *can* get tuna-only tuna for a great price. Just make sure to keep an eye out for sales and coupons to make this recipe even more budget friendly!

Serves 2–3 people

TUNA SALAD

2 cans tuna

1 batch of mayo
{see p. 21}

½ medium onion,
finely diced

½ cucumber, cut into
bite-size pieces

1 medium tomato, cut
into bite-size pieces

1 tsp. apple cider vinegar

1 tsp. mustard

½ tsp. garlic powder

1 Tbsp. basil

salt and pepper

How-to:

- Drain your tuna cans and add tuna into a medium mixing bowl. Use a fork to break it into pieces.

- Add in the rest of your ingredients. Stir well.

- *Boom!* It's done—easy, quick, and yummy tuna!

AUTHOR'S NOTE:

One of my favorite ways to serve this is with a side of cauliflower rice {see directions on page 166}, and I'll make Mr. Not-So-Paleo some white rice. With a small addition of the cauliflower rice, you'll get dinner with minimal to no fuss!

I happen to live with a man obsessed with seafood. Trust me, this is not an understatement; if he could eat it all day every day, I'm guessing he would. Needless to say, I needed an easy inexpensive way to keep him a happy man. I believe this recipe has fit the bill for everyone!

Serves 1 person

½ lb. medium shrimp, raw

coconut oil, butter, or ghee

½ small onion, finely diced

1 clove of garlic, finely chopped

juice from 1 fresh lemon

1½ tsp. parsley

salt and pepper

cauliflower rice {see p. 166} or zucchini noodles {p. 37}

EASY SHRIMP

How-to:

- Peel and devein your shrimp, if it hasn't been already. I generally buy shrimp deveined and will peel off the shell myself.

- In a large skillet, start melting your fat of choice on medium heat. Put in your onions and garlic and let them cook for a few minutes. You don't need a lot of color—you just want them softened slightly.

- Add your shrimp to the skillet and let it start to cook. Add in the lemon juice, sprinkle on your parsley, and add a dash of salt and pepper.

- When your shrimp are a few seconds from being done {they will be a pretty pink color}, turn off your stove and move skillet to a different burner. The heat from your skillet will finish cooking them all the way through. That way you don't have tough overdone shrimp!

- Plate the shrimp over a bed of cauliflower rice or zucchini noodles and enjoy!

AUTHOR'S NOTE:

You can also serve this with white rice {which is how Mr. Not-So-Paleo eats it}!

I love this salmon. It's actually one of the first dishes I added to the blog, so I have a soft spot for it. This is a simple dish, and it doesn't take much time at all. I'm going to be totally honest with you: I don't eat seafood a lot, so when I do, I like it to be the highest quality I can afford. I'll actually hold off on getting it until I can afford the best because I want beautiful, flavorful fish. I generally buy wild-caught fish. I know it's not budget-friendly, but it's worth it. If you can't afford the fresh wild-caught fish, try looking for it frozen, which will generally be cheaper and readily available.

Serves 1–2 people

ALMOND SALMON

1 lb. salmon

a handful of raw almonds

pepper

½ tsp. parsley

lemon juice

2 tsp. butter or ghee

lemon wedges

How-to:

- Preheat your oven to 350°F.

- Rinse your salmon under cool water and pat it dry. Run your fingers up and down the salmon to check for bones. Leaving the skin on or off is completely your choice. I've cooked it both ways.

- Place the salmon in a baking dish.

- Put your almonds into a sandwich bag. Use a mug or something heavy to crush them into pieces. This is a great way to get any pent-up anger out, so really go to town on these bad boys—they can handle it!

- Sprinkle the almonds evenly over the top of the salmon and then sprinkle on some pepper and parsley.

- Squeeze a little bit of lemon juice over the whole thing and dot the top of the salmon with your butter or ghee.

- Bake for 10–15 minutes, or until done to your liking. Around here we like it a light pink on the inside and flaky. Just be careful not to overcook it because it will get dry quickly.

- Serve with some lemon wedges on the side and enjoy!

This recipe is super fun because it has a warm and a cold component to it! I love that play on temperature when eating {and yes, I learned it from Mum}—it brings out the flavors of each side and takes what would be ordinary to something a little more, well, epic. This is great for the summertime, and you can grill your shrimp instead of sautéing it on the stove. When it comes to buying your shrimp, you have a few options: You can go raw and not peeled, raw deveined and not peeled, raw deveined and peeled, or precooked. Honestly, if you can afford to go deveined and peeled, that's the way to go! You don't want to be sitting there peeling the shell and removing the vein. Trust me, it can take forever. However, sometimes I'll find cocktail shrimp {cooked shrimp} on sale for a stellar price, so I'll buy it and reheat it in the skillet. It's not cheating; it's saving you time, which is equally as important as saving money. I wouldn't recommend buying it precooked and then grilling it because you'll end up with tough, icky shrimp! Ready for the recipe?

Serves 1–2 people

SUMMER SHRIMP SALAD

Cold component:

2 medium tomatoes, chopped into bite-size pieces

½ medium onion, finely diced

1 medium cucumber, chopped into bite-size pieces

1½ tsp. basil

1 Tbsp. olive oil

juice from ¼ lemon

salt and pepper

Warm component:

½ Tbsp. coconut oil, ghee, or butter

1 lb. medium shrimp

juice from ¼ lemon

1 tsp. parsley

salt and pepper

How-to:

◉ Combine all of the cold component ingredients together in a large mixing bowl and mix well. Place the bowl in the fridge until you're ready for it.

◉ Heat a medium-sized skillet on medium heat with some coconut oil, ghee, or butter.

◉ Once the skillet is heated, add in your shrimp. Here's the trick to not overcooking it: just as the shrimp is turning that pretty pink color that screams "cooked shrimp," turn the heat off, take the skillet off the heat, an[d] the heat from the pan to finish cooking it for [a] minute or so.

Directions continue[d]

@ Right before the shrimp is finished, add in your lemon juice, parsley, and salt and pepper. Mix it all together in the pan.

@ Grab your bowl from the fridge with all your veggies. Add the shrimp and all it's juices into the bowl and mix everything together. Serve immediately.

@ Enjoy!

AUTHOR'S NOTE:

This dish works well served with cauliflower rice or white rice, but make sure to season it with parsley and basil to carry the flavors over from one to the other.

I rarely eat fish, as most of you guys know. So when I do spend the money on good-quality wild-caught fish, I want it to be light and airy and easy. I also want to taste the fish and not a million other ingredients. You'll notice in this recipe that I used haddock, but you can use any white fish you like. Heck, I think this recipe would actually work with almost any kind of fish! With fish, I like to serve an equally light but filling side dish. I'd highly recommend the sweet potato rounds {see page 112} or confetti rice {page 180}.

Serves 2 people

HADDOCK

1 lb. haddock filets

½ tsp. parsley

½ lemon, cut into thin slices

salt and pepper

How-to:

- Preheat your oven to 350°F.

- Rinse the filets in cool water and pat dry. Run your fingers over the filet in both directions to check for any bones.

- Place the fish in an oven-safe dish with sides.

- Sprinkle your parsley evenly over the haddock and then lay slices of lemon across the top. Sprinkle the fish with a little salt and pepper to taste {I like a fair amount}.

- Bake for 15–20 minutes, until the fish is opaque and slightly flaky. Be careful not to overcook or your fish can get dry.

- Enjoy!

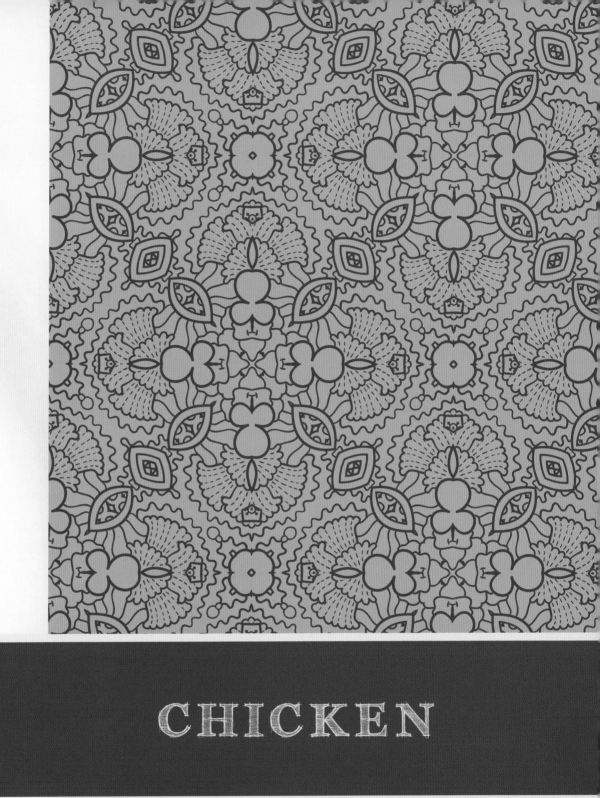

CHICKEN

Want to talk about a yummy multiuse recipe? This is the one for you! I adore this chicken fajita recipe. It's great as is or with a side of roasted carrots, on top of a salad, on top of cauliflower rice, and the list goes on and on! So don't be afraid to mix and match this with other things. And as a quick note: I didn't make this super spicy, in case you don't like spice. If you're in love with all things spicy and tongue-burning, add in some jalapeños, hot sauce, chili flakes, and so on to make it extra awesome. This also pairs well with guacamole {see page 32} and salsa {page 31}.

Serves 2–4 people

1 Tbsp. butter or ghee

2 lbs. boneless skinless chicken breast

1 {16-oz.} bag frozen peppers and onions

½ tsp. garlic powder

2 Tbsp. apple cider vinegar

2 Tbsp. chili powder

1½ Tbsp. basil

1 Tbsp. cumin

salt and pepper

CHICKEN FAJITAS

How-to:

- Heat a large skillet on medium heat with butter or ghee.

- While it's heating, chop up your chicken and drop it into the pan to start cooking. When the chicken is cooked about half-way through, add in your bag of frozen peppers and onions.

- Add in your garlic powder, apple cider vinegar, chili powder, basil, cumin, and salt and pepper. Mix it up well.

- Let everything finish cooking. Taste and adjust seasoning if needed.

- It's done. Talk about a quick dinner!

AUTHOR'S NOTE:

To make this dinner even faster, pre-chop your chicken a night or two before. That way when you come home from work, you can just dump everything into the skillet and let it cook!

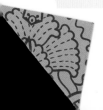

When I was a kid, my sister used to order chicken alfredo a lot when we went out to dinner. And I confess, when she wasn't looking, I'd snag a piece of chicken because I loved the combination of chicken and a creamy sauce. And then one day I thought to myself, there has to be a way to give you that level of yum without the work and extra-ingredient buying. So here you have it: an easy creamy chicken recipe that will fill you up and make you one happy camper, minus the camping!

Serves 2 people

CREAMY CHICKEN

coconut oil, butter,
or ghee

1 medium onion,
medium-diced

½ {8-oz.} container white
mushrooms; cleaned,
de-stemmed, and chopped

1½ lbs. chicken breast, diced
into bite-size pieces
*{or 1 medium chicken
breast per person}*

2 batches of mayo, divided
{see p. 21}

1 tsp. basil

salt and pepper

½ {10-oz.} container
cherry tomatoes,
washed and halved

zucchini noodles
{see p. 37}

How-to:

- Heat a large skillet on medium-high with coconut oil, butter, or ghee. Add your onion and mushrooms and let them start to soften.

- After a few minutes, add your chicken and allow it to cook through. While the chicken is cooking, make your first batch of mayo.

- Once your chicken is cooked, add in your basil and salt and pepper. Turn off the heat and give it a nice mix.

- Right after you turn off the heat, add your first batch of mayo into the skillet and mix it well. This is going to slightly cook your egg and create some thickness in the sauce.

- Set the skillet aside for a moment and make your second batch of mayo. Add the mayo and your cherry tomatoes to the skillet and mix well. Taste and adjust seasoning if needed.

- Serve on a bed of zucchini noodles and enjoy!

L et's talk easy, filling, and easy. Did I mention easy? This is the perfect meal for anyone who doesn't want to cook or is too busy to cook. I think we all fall into one of those categories at least a few times a week! Sometimes I think I'm even a mix of both of them at the same time. Anyway, this lemon chicken not only tastes good, but it's also filling and is an all-in-one meal. Just serve with a side salad or a starch if you want one and you're good to go!

Serves 2–3 people

LEMON CHICKEN

1½ lbs. chicken breasts

salt and pepper

2 zucchini, sliced into ⅛-inch rounds

1 medium onion, thinly sliced

1–2 tsp. basil

1 tsp. oregano

1 lemon, cut into ¼-inch rounds

juice from ¼ lemon

How-to:

◎ Preheat your oven to 375°F.

◎ Wash your chicken, pat it dry, and place it in the bottom of a baking dish {one with sides to it}. Sprinkle some salt and pepper on top of the chicken.

◎ Lay your zucchini rounds and onion slices on top of your chicken. Sprinkle on your oregano, basil, and a little more pepper.

◎ Lay the lemon slices on top of everything, and spritz on the lemon juice.

◎ Cover the whole thing tightly with aluminum foil and place in oven.

◎ Bake for 30–40 minutes or until the chicken is cooked all the way through.

◎ Remove the foil. But be careful. There's a lot of steam inside and you could easily burn your fingers—and nothing ruins a yummy chicken dinner quicker than burnt fingers!

◎ Serve up and make sure to save the leftovers. It tastes just as yummy the next day.

◎ Enjoy!

If you've ever been on my blog, you might have noticed I have a big obsession with chicken salad. I love all kinds of chicken salad and love to experiment with new ingredients in it. This is my basic, easy-to-make, any-night-of-the-week chicken salad. You can totally use this as a base chicken salad and add to it and expand on it {and check out the blog for more ideas}. Don't forget, chicken salad is yummy any time of year—it doesn't have to be a summer dish, and you can serve it warm, room temperature, or straight out of the fridge.

Serves 2–4 people

2½ cups diced or shredded
cooked chicken
{any kind of chicken cooked
by any method}

1 small onion, finely diced

½ large green apple,
diced into bite-size pieces

½ cup raisins

1 Tbsp. mustard
{I like classic yellow mustard}

1–2 batches of mayo
{see p. 21}

1 tsp. rosemary

2 Tbsp. apple cider vinegar
or lemon juice

salt and pepper

CHICKEN SALAD

How-to:

@ Add your chicken to a very large mixing bowl. {How you cook your chicken, if it's fresh or leftover, or if it's white or dark doesn't matter. It's whatever you have right now and is easy to use.}

@ Add in your onion, apple, raisins, and mustard and start to mix it a little. Then add the mayo in. {I say 1–2 batches of mayo because it depends on how "wet" you like your chicken salad. I personally don't like it drowned in mayo, but you might, which is totally cool! So I suggest that the first time you make it, have enough ingredients on hand to make 2 batches of mayo and then make 1 batch and see if you need more. You'll know for the future how much you need!}

@ Add in the rest of your ingredients and mix well. Taste test for seasoning and adjust as needed.

@ Serve and enjoy!

AUTHOR'S NOTE:

The beauty of this recipe is that it easily goes from paleo to non-paleo based on how someone eats it, which makes this the best dish to bring to a party!

I know, I know. Stuffed chicken can be one of two things: boring or difficult to make. I promise this is neither. It's yummy, easy and fool proof. This is one of those elegant looking easy meals that you could serve when you've got family over and it'll look like it took you a long time to make. Serve this with either a starch or panzanella salad {see page 91} for something fresh!

Serves 2 people

STUFFED CHICKEN

ghee, butter, or coconut oil

1 small onion, medium-diced

½ {8-oz.} container mushrooms; de-stemmed, washed, and chopped

1 {3-oz.} sausage
{I'd suggest a spicy one}

½ cup frozen spinach or kale

1 tsp. rosemary

1 tsp. apple cider vinegar

salt and pepper

2 chicken breasts
{about 1¼ lbs. total}

How-to:

@ Preheat your oven to 350°F.

@ Heat a skillet on medium-high heat with ghee, butter, or coconut oil. Add in your onion and mushrooms. Let them start to cook a little and soften.

@ Remove the casing from your sausage and add it into the skillet. Let that start to cook. When it's almost done, add in your spinach or kale, rosemary, apple cider vinegar, and a sprinkling of salt and pepper.

@ Allow to finish cooking. Once it's cooked, remove it into a separate bowl or plate in order to allow it to cool faster.

@ Rinse your chicken under cool water and pat dry. Then you're going to butterfly your chicken. It's easy to do I promise. Just make a cut into the chicken along the side. Keep cutting until you're almost all the way through. You'll be able to then open up the chicken like a book. It's called butterflying because the chicken almost resembles a butterfly when it's open.

@ Scoop about 2–3 tablespoons of your filling onto one side of the chicken. If you can fit a little bit more, feel free! But don't overstuff the chicken or it will cook unevenly.

@ Refold the chicken so it looks like it did before cutting it open. Place in a baking tray with sides. Sprinkle some more pepper on top and cover the chicken tightly with aluminum foil. Cook for 20–30 minutes or until the chicken is cooked all the way through.

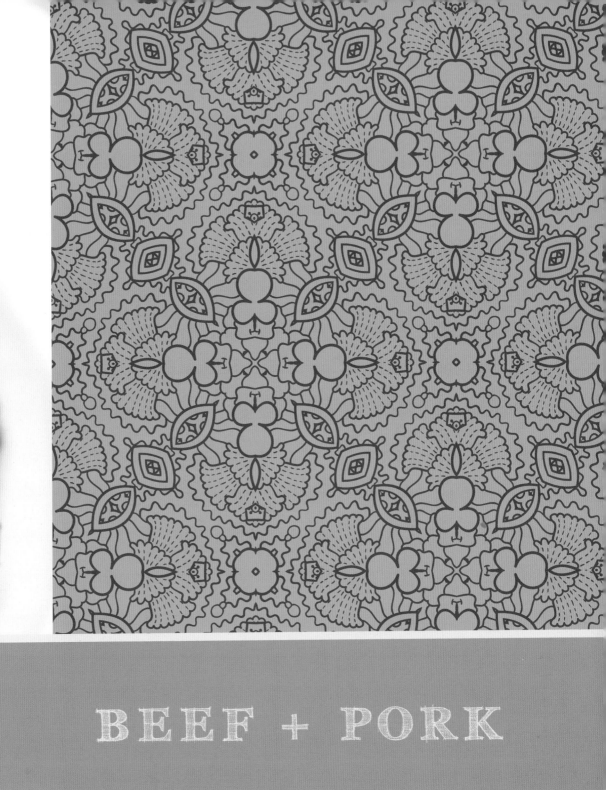

BEEF + PORK

love burgers. Seriously, they're one of the greatest things ever created. Whenever we go out to eat, my eye zeros right in on that lovely section! Why? Because burgers work for pretty much everyone and every occasion. When I got married, I think if I could have had a burger, I would have; they're that good. Best thing? You don't need a grill to make them. That's right—you just need a skillet and a stove. This particular burger recipe can be done with any kind of meat: beef, pork, lamb, bison, venison, and so on. But make sure you're burger is cooked through to whatever is appropriate for that particular meat.

Serves 2–3 people

BURGERS

butter, ghee, coconut oil, or bacon fat

1 lb. ground meat
{I used ground pork for the picture}

2 white button mushrooms; de-stemmed, cleaned, and finely chopped

½ tsp. oregano

salt and pepper

How-to:

◉ Get a large skillet heating on medium to medium-low heat with butter, ghee, coconut oil, or bacon fat.

◉ Put your ground meat into a medium mixing bowl. Add your mushrooms, oregano, and salt and pepper.

◉ Mix well with your hands. But don't overmix—that will make the meat tough.

◉ Make the burgers any size you'd like and round them out into patties. Drop them into the skillet as you form them. {I personally am a fan of the smaller burgers—maybe a little bigger than a slider. They cook quicker that size and are easier to eat!}

◉ Cook evenly on both sides and serve with your favorite sides. May I suggest some coleslaw {see page 108} or maybe a panzanella salad {see page 91}!

AUTHOR'S NOTE:

You can absolutely form these little lovelies in advance before cooking. Just make the meat mixture, form them into patties, and place on a plate. Cover the plate with foil and keep chilled in the fridge. Then take them out about ten minutes before cooking so they can come to room temperature, which allows them to cook more evenly. My dad is famous for doing this when he grills in the summer—so thank you, Dad, for the great idea!

C ube steak is a fun piece of meat. It's cheap {because a lot of people don't buy it}, and it's yummy. Now a fair warning: this is an insanely easy and fast recipe. I've done the whole "breading" thing and dredging it in, but let's be honest for a second. I hate dishes, and, well, that whole process requires more dishes and more of a mess. Not to mention egg-goo plus almond flour on your hands is not as fun as it sounds {at least for me}. So this is my compromise because Mr. Not-So-Paleo *loves* cube steak. Always has, always will. Me? I like it too, now that I've simplified it.

Serves 1 person

CUBE STEAK

about 1 Tbsp. butter, ghee, coconut oil, or bacon fat

dried herb of choice
{I like rosemary or parsley}

salt and pepper

1 cube steak

How-to:

- Heat a large skillet on medium-high with butter, ghee, coconut oil, or bacon fat {bacon fat makes it the yummiest}.

- While that's heating, sprinkle your herb of choice and salt and pepper on one side of the cube steak. I try to do this while it's still in the package because I hate messing up an extra cutting board just to season something. But if you can't manage that in the packaging, don't worry—just lay it out flat on a cutting board and you're in business!

- With a pair of tongs, put the steaks seasoned side down into the hot skillet.

- While the steak starts to get all pretty and yummy on that side, season the other side with more of your herb of choice and salt and pepper.

- Flip the steak over a few minutes later and let it cook on the other side until it's done to your liking.

- Enjoy!

AUTHOR'S NOTE:

I like to eat this for breakfast because it's a great way to get a good, filling meal in my belly quickly. However, when I'm making this for dinner, I like to add a lot of caramelized onions {see page 27} on top!

Steak and peppers is a classic. A classic that barely anyone ever eats. I have no idea why so many people don't make this at home on a weekly basis! It's ridiculously easy and uses a cheap cut of meat that is frequently on sale. {Bonus round: you can also get shaved pork if that floats your boat more than shaved steak.} Not to mention this is very {let me repeat: very} versatile and cheap! You can pair this with almost any side dish, and the non-paleos in your life aren't going to be able to say no. It even rocks as leftovers in eggs for breakfast the next morning. I could probably go on and on about how much I love this recipe, but I'll just give you the how-tos and the what-you-need and let you go to town!

Serves 2–3 people

about 1 Tbsp. coconut oil, ghee, or butter

¾ {16-oz.} bag frozen peppers and onions

1 lb. shaved steak

1 tsp. basil
{or other herb of choice}

2 tsp. apple cider vinegar

salt and pepper

STEAK AND PEPPERS

How-to:

- Heat a large skillet on medium heat with coconut oil, ghee, or butter.

- Add your frozen peppers and onions to start cooking.

- When the peppers and onions are almost completely done, add in your shaved steak and mix everything around. I like to use two forks to separate the shaved steak as it cooks; it has a tendency to stick together because it's so thin.

- Add in your basil, apple cider vinegar, and salt and pepper. Mix well.

- Taste test for seasoning, adjust if needed, and you're done!

AUTHOR'S NOTE:

I personally think this rocks with the roasted cauliflower salad {see page 84} or roasted sweet potatoes or carrots! And if you're serving this to paleos and non-paleos, simply let them pick how they'd like to eat it. They can pair this with your paleo sides or they can choose to put it on a bun and eat it as a sandwich!

...e guys are way too awesome for words to describe. They're an awesome mixture of fun meets ...egant. Your kids are going to like how they can eat them with their hands, and you'll love the ...flavor. Not to mention, they're easy! To make them even easier, make your filling a day or two beforehand {or even weeks ahead and freeze it}.

ZUCCHINI BOATS

Makes 6–8 boats
{2 per person}

3–4 zucchini

olive oil

salt and pepper

ghee or butter

1 medium onion

5–6 white button
mushrooms

4 {3-oz.} spicy sausages

1 {14-oz.} can
diced tomatoes

1 tsp. rosemary

How-to:

◎ Preheat your oven to 350°F.

◎ Wash and cut the ends off your zucchini. Slice them lengthwise down the center and use a spoon to hollow them out.

◎ Place your hollowed out zucchini in a baking dish, bowl side up. Drizzle with a little bit of olive oil and sprinkle with salt and pepper. Place them in the oven and bake for 15 minutes, until they've started to roast and soften.

◎ While those are roasting, heat a skillet on medium-high with some ghee or butter {I like butter}. Finely dice your onion and mushrooms and add them into the pan. Let them sauté together for a few minutes.

◎ While that's going, take the casing off your sausages and crumble them into the skillet to start cooking.

◎ Drain your can of diced tomatoes and add them into the skillet along with the rosemary and some salt and pepper.

◎ Once your zucchini are cooked, scoop the filling into the boats and let those bake for an additional 10 minutes in your oven. Then serve!

This is one of my family's favorite dishes that I make. These stuffed peppers are simple and yummy—two major hallmarks of any great dinner! This recipe can get expensive if you're cooking for a large crowd. If that's the case, use green bell peppers. They're almost a dollar per pound cheaper! I also keep costs low by serving half a pepper per person and then adding some kind of side dish to serve alongside. A nice green salad works, or try sweet potato rounds {see page 112} or even roasted cauliflower salad {see page 84}.

Serves 2–4 people

STUFFED PEPPERS

2 red or orange bell peppers
{Mr. Not-So-Paleo suggests orange}

olive oil

salt and pepper

coconut oil, ghee,
or butter

1 medium onion,
finely diced

1 lb. ground beef

1 {14-oz.} can diced
tomatoes, drained

1 Tbsp. Italian seasoning

1 Tbsp. basil

2–3 Tbsp. apple
cider vinegar

How-to:

@ Preheat your oven to 400°F.

@ Cut your peppers in half lengthwise and clean them out. {I prefer lengthwise to cutting off the top because you can get more filling in and you can divide a pepper between two people.} Place them on a baking sheet and drizzle with a little bit of olive oil and salt and pepper. Bake for 15–20 minutes or until they've started to soften.

@ While those are roasting, heat a large skillet on medium heat with coconut oil, ghee, or butter. Add in your onions and let them start to soften for a few minutes. Then add in your ground meat and let it start to cook.

@ When your meat is about halfway cooked, add in your diced tomatoes, Italian seasoning, basil, apple cider vinegar, and some salt and pepper. Stir well and let it finish cooking.

@ Once your filling is cooked and your peppers are roasted drop your oven's temperature down to 350°F and remove the peppers from the oven.

@ Fill your peppers with as much filling as you'd like and bake them for 20–30 minutes.

AUTHOR'S NOTES:

If you're a rice eater or you have rice eaters in your family, you can add some rice to these to make them more traditional! I'd suggest adding a half to a full cup of rice per every pound of ground meat that you use. Unless you're cooking for Mr. Not-So-Paleo, in which case of course you double or triple the recommended rice amount!

This meal is dedicated to my very own Mr. Not-So-Paleo. We both needed a comfort meal of sorts way back when, and I came up with this as a result. It stuck and has been a favorite of his {and mine!} ever since. The best part is it's amazingly easy for the amount of happiness it brings you. If steak doesn't give you comfort but pork or chicken do, swap the steak out for what you like. Remember, this is a comfort meal, so make sure whatever you put in it is going to make you want to snuggle into the couch and sigh with happiness.

Serves 2 people

COMFORT MEAL

1 sweet potato

olive oil

rosemary

salt and pepper

coconut oil, butter, or ghee

1 medium onion, medium-diced

½ {8-oz.} container mushrooms; cleaned, de-stemmed, and chopped

1 lb. steak, cut into bite-size pieces

2 Tbsp. apple cider vinegar

½ tsp. dried or fresh basil

½ tsp. rosemary

...ium tomato, ...dium-diced

How-to:

- Preheat your oven to 375°F.

- Wash and chop up your sweet potato with skin on into bite-size pieces. Drizzle on some olive oil and then sprinkle on rosemary and salt and pepper. Toss it all together and spread in a single layer on a baking sheet. Roast them for 30–40 minutes, until they're cooked and crispy {but not burnt}.

- While the sweet potatoes are cooking, heat a large skillet on medium heat with some coconut oil, butter, or ghee. Add in your onions and mushrooms to start cooking. If they cook faster than you need them to, turn the skillet to low and let it just keep warm until you're ready for the next step.

- When your sweet potatoes are about 15 minutes away from being done, cut up your steak and add it into the skillet along with the apple cider vinegar, basil, rosemary, and a little more salt and pepper. Let it cook until the steak is done to your liking and then turn off the stove.

- When your sweet potatoes are done, add them into the skillet and give the mixture a good stir. Serve it in bowls and sprinkle your tomatoes evenly on top.

- It's all done. Enjoy!

AUTHOR'S NOTE:

On top of this, I like to drizzle a slightly thinner mayo {see page 21} seasoned with parsley, salt, and pepper. And if you're not a fan of sweet potatoes or don't have any, swap it out for roasted butternut squash instead {see page 111}. It's equally as yummy!

This recipe is another blog favorite, so I had to include it! I've received emails from people saying this was non-paleo approved, husband approved, and picky kid approved. {Husband- and kid-approved recipes are the best compliments a girl can get!} Needless to say, this is a staple and a classic in my house. Why do we love this recipe so much? Because it's a great compromise for paleos and non-paleos. When you serve this for friends and family who aren't paleo, I bet you a dollar they'll have no idea it is paleo. So go on—make this for dinner tonight. I'm guessing you've got most of the stuff in your house right now. {Bonus, right?}

OVERSIZED MEATBALLS WITH SAUCE AND GREEN BEANS

Serves 2–3 people

coconut oil, ghee, or butter

1 lb. ground pork

½ medium onion, finely diced

½ tsp. cumin

salt and pepper

1 medium onion

2 carrots

2 tsp. dried oregano
{or dried thyme}

2 tsp. dried rosemary
{or basil}

1 tsp. cumin

1 tsp. chili powder

3–4 Tbsp. apple cider vinegar, plus more
{or balsamic vinegar}

1 {28-oz.} can crushed tomatoes

2–3 cups chopped frozen green beans

How-to:

- Heat a skillet {with high sides} on medium-high with some coconut oil, ghee, or butter.

- While the skillet is heating, combine your pork, onion, cumin, and salt and pepper and mix it all together well. Then create meatballs the size of golf balls and place them in the skillet as you form them.

- Let them sit for 3–4 minutes per side. You only need these to brown, not cook all the way through.

- While they're browning, medium-dice your onion and carrots. Remove your meatballs from the skillet, place them on a plate, and set it aside.

- Use a spatula to scrape any bits at the bottom of the skillet. Add your diced onion and carrots. Add a smidge of apple cider vinegar to let any yummy bits at the bottom of the pan loosen up.

- After a few minutes, add in your oregano, rosemary, cumin, and chili powder, coating the veggies evenly and letting the spices start to warm up a bit.

- Add in 3–4 tablespoons of your apple cider vinegar. If you don't want a tangy sauce, don't add as much in—just a tablespoon or so.

- Add in your crushed tomatoes and a little more salt and pepper. Give the sauce a good stir.

- Then nestle your meatballs back into the sauce, making sure to also add the juices back in that collected on the plate.

- Set the stove on low and cover skillet, allowing a little room for steam to escape. {If your skillet doesn't have a lid, don't fret! Just use a little bit of aluminum foil laid loosely on top.} Let it cook for 30–45 minutes, or until the meatballs are cooked through.

- About 15 minutes before it's done, add your green beans on top, re-cover, and let the dish finish cooking.

AUTHOR'S NOTE:

I've also done this dish with roasted fresh green beans {see page 54} when they're in season, and it is yummy that way! I've also just used a Steamfresh bag of green beans, which also works beautifully. Additionally, if you don't like green beans, you can omit them or use zucchini noodles!

Pork tenderloin is a cut of meat that borderlines being expensive, unless you can get it on sale. To make it even more affordable, I've mixed in a few things with it. The nice part is that this easy filling weeknight meal only takes a short time to make! Enjoy this with cauliflower rice {see page 166}, butternut squash {page 111 or 116}, or zucchini noodles {page 37}.

Serves 2 people

PORK TENDERLOIN

coconut oil, ghee,
or butter

1 medium onion,
medium-diced

¾ green apple

1 lb. pork tenderloin

2 tsp. rosemary

2 tsp. apple cider vinegar

salt and pepper

How-to:

- Heat a large skillet on medium heat with coconut oil, ghee, or butter. Add in your onions and let them start to soften.

- While that's happening, chop your ¾ apple into bite-size pieces and add that into the skillet as well. The extra quarter of the apple is a snack for you and whatever helpers you have in the kitchen {for me it's normally the dog—she loves her apples}.

- While those are getting all friendly, cut your tenderloin into bite-size pieces. Remove any fat or sinew if you don't like eating it {I don't, so I trim it down}.

- Add the pork tenderloin into the pan along with the rosemary, apple cider vinegar, and salt and pepper.

- Allow it to finish cooking and then serve.

- Enjoy!

L asagna is fun to eat and is yummy, filling, and hearty. Serve this with a side salad and you've got yourself one stellar dinner. Not to mention, you'll impress friends and family with how creative and skilled you are. Trust me, you've got mad skills, and this is the perfect recipe to show them off with.

Serves 2–4 people

ZUCCHINI LASAGNA

coconut oil, ghee,
or butter

3 {3-oz.} sausages

3 zucchini

1 batch tomato sauce
{see p. 43}

slivered almonds
{optional}

How-to:

- Preheat oven to 375°F.

- In a small skillet, add a little bit of coconut oil, ghee, or butter and set heat to medium-high.

- Remove your sausages from the casing and crumble into the pan. Let it cook until it's completely cooked. Turn off the stove and set the skillet off to the side.

- Thinly slice your zucchini lengthwise so it almost looks like a lasagna noodle. It's okay if one or two break in half; you can still use it!

- Spoon a little bit of sauce in the bottom of your lasagna pan {I use a 10¾ × 8½ pan; 2½-quart size}. Spread the sauce into a thin layer.

- Lay the zucchini lengthwise in the pan, letting each piece overlap sightly. Make sure the zucchini covers the pan completely.

- Spread on an even layer of sauce and sprinkle half of your sausage across. If you'd like to add slivered almonds {for crunch}, sprinkle it on now.

- Layer more zucchini on top, just like you did before. Spread more sauce on and sprinkle the rest of your sausage on top.

- Cover tightly with aluminum foil and bake for 15 minutes. Then pull it out of the oven, remove the foil, and bake for another 15 minutes or until done. It's done when you can insert a steak knife into the zucchini and it goes in easy.

AUTHOR'S NOTE:

If you eat dairy, you can sprinkle shredded raw cheese on top of the lasagna for the last ten minutes of cooking. I think provolone or cheddar both work well. It will be nice and crunchy and cheesy all at the same time.

It's no secret that I used to love burritos. When I was a hair stylist, my friends and I would frequent one place in particular that made the best burritos around—they were so good we'd ask the husbands of stylists to pick up burritos for us for lunch. Nowadays, I'm not doing the whole burrito thing, but I miss the flavors and textures! My solution? A broken-down burrito. It has all my personal favorite ingredients, but you can add whatever makes you want to dance around because you're so happy.

Serves 2–3 people

BROKEN-DOWN BURRITO

½ medium head of cauliflower

grass-fed butter, ghee, or coconut oil

1 small onion, medium-diced

1 batch of mayo
{see p. 21}

fresh lemon juice

1 lb. steak, cut into bite-size pieces

1 tsp. cumin

½ tsp. garlic powder

salt and pepper

2 small tomatoes, cut into bite-size pieces

lettuce

1 tsp. parsley

How-to:

- Make cauliflower rice: Cut your half head of cauliflower into florets, add to a blender or food processor, and pulse until it looks like "rice." Then move it into a microwaveable bowl, cover with plastic wrap, and microwave for 4–5 minutes.

- While that's in the microwave, heat a large skillet on medium heat with butter, ghee, or coconut oil. Add in your onion and let it start to soften. By now your microwave has probably gone off. That's fine. Leave the cauliflower rice in there for the moment!

- Right around this time I make my mayo, thinning it out with lemon juice a little so it's like a dressing.

- Add steak, cumin, garlic powder, and a sprinkle of salt and pepper to your skillet.

- While your steak is cooking, chop your tomatoes into bite-size pieces and chop up your lettuce. Reheat your cauliflower rice for one minute in the microwave. When your steak is done, turn off the stove and set it aside to another burner.

- Pull the cauliflower rice out, add in a few teaspoons of butter or ghee, your parsley, and a sprinkling of salt and pepper. Mix well.

@ Now it's time to assemble: you can add as much or as little of each item! On a plate, start with a layer of lettuce and then cauliflower rice, steak and onions, and fresh tomatoes on top. Then drizzle with your mayo dressing and serve!

@ Enjoy!

AUTHOR'S NOTE:

You can prep your cauliflower rice the night before and reheat before serving. You can also pre-chop your veggies to save you some time when cooking.

If you are serving this for family, it might be fun to serve this family-style and let people assemble their own broken-down burritos!

This is one hearty dinner. It's a little involved, but the effort is worth it, trust me. I don't make this weekly; it's one of my non-special-occasion special meals. You know the nights I'm talking about, when you want something a little more than basic, but you really have no reason to celebrate. This is the perfect meal for those occasions!

Serves 2–3 people

6 medium-sized portobello mushroom caps

olive oil

salt and pepper

coconut oil, butter, or ghee

1 medium onion, medium-diced

1 lb. ground beef or pork

½ {8-oz.} bag frozen pepper strips

1 {14-oz.} can diced tomatoes, drained

1 Tbsp. rosemary

1 tsp. basil

½ tsp. garlic powder

almond flour
{optional}

STUFFED PORTOBELLO MUSHROOMS

How-to:

- Preheat your oven to 375°F.

- Take the stems off your mushrooms and use the side of a spoon to scrape the inside gills off it {the black stuff}. Then use a damp towel to wipe off the top.

- Place them on a baking sheet with the part you're going to fill facing up. Drizzle them with some olive oil and sprinkle with salt and pepper. Roast in the oven for 15–20 minutes or until you can pierce them easily with a steak knife.

- While these are roasting, heat a large skillet on medium heat with coconut oil, butter, or ghee and add in your onions to start to soften.

- After a few minutes, add in your ground meat and let it cook. When it's halfway cooked, add in the rest of your ingredients, except the almond flour, along with a little extra salt and pepper. Mix well.

- Let the mixture finish cooking. Turn off the stove and set the skillet aside.

- When your mushroom caps are done, stuff them with as much filling as you'd like. If desired, sprinkle the top with a little bit of almond flour.

- Turn your oven down to 350°F and bake your mushrooms for 10–15 minutes. If you're using almond flour, allow brown slightly on top. Serve and enjoy!

Elizabeth McGaw

There's this well-kept secret that I love meat loaf. Why is it a secret? Because I used to be horrible at making it. It used to be either too dry or too wet or just not there flavor-wise. I hadn't made a mini meat loaf in so long either because I attempted it a few times when Mr. Not-So-Paleo and I lived in Providence, and let's just say Mr. Not-So-Paleo never asked for seconds. And he never asked for it again. But the good news? I have defeated the mini meat loaf {in a good way} and finally made some that are so yummy Mr. Not-So-Paleo will even eat them the next day as a snack! I like to make these as a dinner {I normally do three or four per person in that case}, or I like to have them on hand throughout the week as a snack or for breakfast and lunch! To make these I use a nonstick twelve-muffin tin.

Makes 12 mini
meat loaves

ghee, butter, or
coconut oil

1 medium carrot,
finely diced

1 medium onion,
finely diced

1 stalk of celery,
finely diced

2 Tbsp. parsley

salt and pepper

cumin

1 large egg,
slightly beaten

1½ lbs. ground beef

MINI MEAT LOAVES

How-to:

- Get your oven preheated to 400°F.

- Heat a medium skillet with ghee, butter, or coconut oil and add your veggies. Let them start to sweat and get all happy. Once they're done, add them into a mixing bowl and allow to cool.

- If necessary, grease your muffin tin. Then chop up your parsley and add it into the mixing bowl with the veggies.

- Add the rest of the ingredients to the mixing bowl. Get your hands in there and mix it well.

- Fill your muffin tin with the filling, nearly all the way to the top.

- Bake in your oven for roughly 20–25 minutes or until cooked all the way through. {Cooking time will vary based on the kind of meat and the size of your muffin tin.}

AUTHORS' NOTE:

You can use any ground meat in these. Make sure you adjust your cooking time to accommodate your ground meat of choice.

Shepherd's pie is a classic. This warm, hearty meal is great in the winter. Not so much in the summer because it requires the stove and the oven. But nonetheless, it's amazing. It takes the same amount of work to make almost any size of batch, so I'd suggest making enough for leftovers. You can even make an extra tray and freeze it instead of baking at the end. You'll have it for an easy meal in the near future! If you don't like sweet potato, not to fret; you can swap it out for squash or something equally as hearty!

Serves 2–4 people

SHEPHERD'S PIE

2 medium sweet potatoes

½ medium onion

coconut oil, butter, or ghee

1 onion, medium-diced

2 carrots, medium-diced

1 lb. ground beef, pork, or lamb

½ {12-oz.} bag cut frozen green beans

1 {14-oz.} can diced tomatoes

1 Tbsp. basil

1 Tbsp. oregano

½ tsp. cumin

1 tsp. rosemary

2 Tbsp. apple cider vinegar

salt and pepper

How-to:

@ Preheat your oven to 350°F.

@ Fill a medium saucepan halfway with water and set it on the stove. Medium-dice your sweet potatoes and add them into the water. Then roughly dice half of an onion and add that into the water as well.

@ Cover your sweet potatoes and onions and put on medium-high heat to boil. Once it has started to boil, turn the heat down a little and prop the lid. You'll know it's done when the sweet potatoes are fork tender {usually takes about 20 minutes}.

@ While your sweet potatoes are getting all cozy in the water, start to cook your filling by heating a large skillet on medium-high with coconut oil, butter, or ghee.

@ Add your onions and carrots into the skillet and let them start to soften for a few minutes. Then add in your ground meat and let it start to cook. Once it's halfway cooked, add in your green beans, diced tomatoes, seasonings, apple cider vinegar, and salt and pepper. Mix it all together and let it finish cooking.

@ Once the mixture is cooked, turn off the stove and let the skillet sit off to the side.

Directions continue on next '

◉ When your sweet potatoes are done, drain the water and add in your favorite fat of choice. Add in some salt and pepper and, if you'd like, an herb or two. Mash to your liking. Taste test and adjust seasoning if needed.

◉ Get a large baking dish {a lasagna pan would work} and fill it first with your ground meat mixture and then layer the mashed sweet potato on top. Make sure your sweet potato layer on top is nice and even. {You might have leftover sweet potato. Save it for lunch tomorrow!}

◉ Bake in the oven for 15–20 minutes or until slightly golden brown on top.

◉ Let it cool for a few minutes, serve, and enjoy!

GRAY AREA
+ SPLURGES

Of course I'm throwing a curveball in the mix. It's me—I live for spicing things up, and not just with chili powder and paprika. I wanted to make sure my friends who eat rice and potato had a little something in here. I also wanted to make sure my friends who like desserts, chocolate, or splurging dollar-wise occasionally had a few recipes to enjoy. As always, have fun with the recipes, and try the truffles!

Now I'm sure you're wondering, "Liz, why are these in the Gray Area + Splurges section?" Excellent question! It's because in order to get good-quality scallops, you'll have to shell out a few dollars. {Get it? Shell out. Hilarious, I know!} I used bay scallops for this dish because they were more affordable, but if different scallops are on sale, use those and adjust your cooking time accordingly. Also, this method creates a bit of a broth with the scallops. Don't throw it out! Freeze it and use it whenever you make your next fish-based soup!

Serves 2 people {or 1 Mr. Not-So-Paleo}

1 lb. bay scallops

3–4 Tbsp. almond flour

½ tsp. parsley

½ tsp. basil

¼ tsp. garlic powder

⅛ tsp. salt

pepper

1 Tbsp. melted butter

fresh lemon juice

BAKED SCALLOPS

How-to:

- Preheat your oven to 375°F.

- Rinse your scallops under cool water and pat dry. Place them into a baking dish with high sides.

- In a small bowl combine your almond flour, parsley, basil, garlic powder, salt, and pepper. Give it a mix with your fingers.

- Drizzle your melted butter over your scallops.

- Sprinkle your almond flour mixture on top of each scallop.

- Bake for 15–20 minutes, until they're cooked all the way through.

- Take scallops out of the oven, spritz with a little bit of lemon juice, serve, and enjoy!

AUTHOR'S NOTE:

The topping on the scallops doesn't get crispy, but if that's something you'd like, you could stick it under the broiler for a few minutes {after the topping has been sprinkled on}, but watch it *very* closely since it can burn and turn icky quickly. Also, if you are allergic to nuts, omit the almond flour and sprinkle the mixture as is on top.

These are cute little appetizers. They provide just enough of an "Oh, this is yummy" to have people excited about what's to come next, which is what an appetizer should do in my book. I also enjoy making these when we need something just a little special. You know what I'm talking about—some days you just want a little something more than a burger and carrot fries, and these are the little cuties to do it for you.

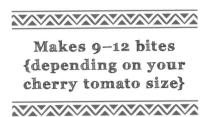

Makes 9–12 bites {depending on your cherry tomato size}

½ {10-oz.} container cherry tomatoes

¼ {8-oz.} container goat cheese

½ tsp. rosemary

pepper

at least 2 tsp. lemon juice

more lemon juice or water

TOMATO BITES

How-to:

- Preheat oven to 350°F.

- Wash your tomatoes and then cut them in half {in the middle, not lengthwise}. Scoop out the inside seeds and guts of each half. {I like to save the seeds/guts and add them to a tomato sauce!}

- Put your tomatoes into a baking dish and set them aside.

- In a separate bowl, combine goat cheese, rosemary, pepper. and a good spritz of lemon juice. Stir it. If it's still very thick and hard to stir, you can add more lemon juice or a little water. I say either lemon juice or water because the lemon juice can become overpowering. The best way to figure out which to use is to taste it a little and decide from there. When you're able to stir the mixture easily but it's still thick, it's the perfect consistency!

- Using a spoon, start to fill your tomatoes with the filling. If you want to make it neat and pretty, fill a ziplock bag with the filling, make a small cut in one of the corners, and use that to pipe in the filling.

- Once the tomato halves are all stuffed, you can sprinkle with extra pepper on top if desired. Bake for 10–15 minutes, until the tomatoes are roasted and warm throughout. Let them cool a little. Serve and enjoy!

Confetti rice is based off one of my Dad's signature side dishes. My sister and I both request it at every available opportunity, and it's the greatest thing in the world to eat at any time. If my dad ever invites you over for dinner, request this tasty little number! Now I know some of you don't eat rice {and are cringing possibly at this recipe}, and that's totally fine! Don't worry about it. Just substitute the white rice with cauliflower rice. Ah, you see what I did there? Made it friendly for both sides of the paleo spectrum! Now go make this side dish tonight with dinner. It's extra tasty with grilled chicken, steak, or shrimp!

Serves 2–4 people

coconut oil, ghee,
or butter

1 medium onion,
finely diced

1 red or orange bell
pepper, finely diced

1 clove of garlic,
finely diced

2 cups cooked white rice
{or 2 cups cauliflower rice}

salt and pepper

1 Tbsp. parsley
{I prefer fresh, but
dried will work too}

CONFETTI RICE

How-to:

@ Heat a skillet on medium-low with coconut oil, ghee, or butter. Add your onion. After a few minutes, add your bell pepper. After about 5 minutes of cooking, add your garlic. The key to this is cooking low and slow. It should take you a good 15 minutes at least.

@ Transfer your onion, pepper, and garlic into your serving bowl. Cover it and leave it be until dinnertime or move on to the next step immediately.

@ Add your cooked rice on top of the onion, pepper, and garlic.

@ Now here's where Dad and I mainly differ. I personally like to add in a little butter, olive oil, or ghee to my rice and mix it in, but he doesn't. It's going to be yummy either way, so pick whichever way makes you happy!

@ Add in salt and pepper and your parsley. Mix everything very well and taste test for seasoning. Adjust if needed.

@ Serve and enjoy!

AUTHOR'S NOTE:

To make your rice even yummier, cook it in chicken stock!

This recipe was originally created because Mr. Not-So-Paleo missed potatoes and was pretty sick of sweet potatoes. So I came up with something that was wicked easy for me to make and was paleo friendly if you're one of my friends who eats white potato. I love to make these as a side dish because they can roast alongside anything that needs to go into the oven. I normally make these for Mr. Not-So-Paleo when I make mini meat loaves {see page 170} or stuffed chicken {page 144}. I pop them into the oven first and then make everything else. By the time the main dish is done, the potatoes are done, and all I have to worry about is making a veggie. See? Super easy, yummy, and, well, fun!

Serves 2–3 people

ROASTED POTATOES

2 lbs. potatoes

olive oil

salt and pepper

basil
{or other herb of choice}

How-to:

◉ Preheat your oven to 375°F.

◉ Wash and chop your potatoes into bite-size pieces. Place them onto a baking tray.

◉ Drizzle some olive oil on top. Then sprinkle salt and pepper and basil over the potatoes.

◉ Toss it all together, place them in a single layer on a baking sheet, and bake for 30–45 minutes or until crispy and cooked through.

◉ Serve and enjoy!

A cookie is more than just a cookie. Even more so when it's a chocolate chip cookie. I'm guessing that as kids most of us were obsessed with some kind of cookie. But now that we're adults and off the grains, what are we to do? Not to fret—I've got a little chocolate chip cookie recipe here to keep us all happy!

Makes 12 cookies

3 Tbsp. butter

1 cup almond flour

2 large eggs

½ tsp. cinnamon

a pinch of salt

1 tsp. raw honey, melted

2 tsp. vanilla

½ cup raisins

½ cup chocolate
{finely chopped or chocolate chips}

CHOCOLATE CHIP COOKIES

How-to:

◎ Preheat your oven to 350°F.

◎ Melt your butter in a small saucepan on medium heat.

◎ While that's melting, put your almond flour in a large bowl. Crack your eggs first in a separate bowl and then add them into the large bowl with the almond flour.

◎ Add all of your ingredients into the bowl, including the melted butter. When it comes to your chocolate, I like to use a bar of chocolate and chop it pretty finely. Half a cup is generally half of a bar of chocolate. Remember—you want your chocolate to have no dairy, nuts, or soy!

◎ Mix it all really well together and use a teaspoon to measure the dough onto a cookie sheet. If you're not using a nonstick sheet, make sure you line it with aluminum foil first.

◎ Wet your fingers a little {I like to leave a little bowl of water next to me} and flatten the cookies out. The nice thing about these cookies is that they don't spread out, so however you place them is how they'll bake. Bake for 6–8 minutes, until golden brown around the edges.

◎ Let them cool for a few minutes and then transfer to a plate to finish cooling. Or you can follow the Liz/Mr. Not-So-Paleo method of eating them super hot and burning your mouth. Either way, they'll be yummy!

◎ Enjoy!

Talk about the easiest, quickest dessert you'll ever come across. This seriously takes maybe ten minutes to make, and then it chills in the fridge until you're ready for it. I make this all the time when we're going places for the holidays because it's so easy and so inexpensive to make, and it's always a hit! Bonus: You can use in-season items to add on top and make it super festive. Or you could be like us and make it for a movie night. {Warning: If you're watching any of the extended editions of *The Lord of the Rings*, you'll need to make two batches per movie.}

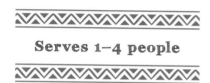

Serves 1–4 people

1 {3-oz.} bar 85% or darker chocolate

½ tsp. vanilla extract

chopped or slivered almonds, raisins, and unsweetened shredded coconut to taste

BARK

How-to:

@ Create a double boiler to melt your chocolate. To do this, find a heat-safe mixing bowl {I like glass or stainless steel} that will nestle nicely on top, or slightly in, a saucepan. Fill the saucepan halfway with water, place the bowl on top, and turn your heat on medium-low. Let the water start to simmer. Remember, you don't want the water to ever boil—keep it at a constant simmer.

@ Chop up your chocolate bar, add it to the double boiler, and let it start to melt. Make sure that you don't have steam coming out the sides of your pot and up the bowl. The fastest way to ruin melted chocolate is to get water on or in it.

@ While the chocolate is getting all melty-melty, line a medium baking sheet with aluminum foil.

@ Add your vanilla extract to the chocolate. Stir it up and then spoon it onto your lined baking sheet. If you decide to pour it straight from the bowl to the tray, make sure you wipe the bottom of the bowl well because condensation will gather on the outside bottom of the bowl. The last thing you want is to get water on your oh-so-pretty chocolate.

@ Spread the chocolate out as thin as you'd like it to be. I normally spread it out to around ¼ inch thick. Then sprinkle on your chopped or slivered almonds, raisins, and unsweetened shredded coconut.

- Place the sheet in the fridge for at least 1 hour until the chocolate hardens. When you're ready to eat it, break it apart with your hands into pieces. If not serving immediately, keep it stored in the fridge and eat when ready.

- Enjoy!

AUTHOR'S NOTE:

This treat does kind of melt on your fingers when eating it—I'd suggest after breaking it into pieces to stick it all in the freezer for 10–15 minutes before eating.

I'm a cookie lover. It's not a big secret that cookies make me happy. Cookies are little round disks of extreme happiness that you can make over and over again. These cookies are similar to the coconut pumpkin muffins on my blog. The muffins were a happy accident that happened in round one of cookie-recipe-creating. So if you're thinking of making either the cookies or the muffins, I'd highly suggest making both because you'll have the ingredients for both already! And remember, if you're not a raisin fan, substitute with whatever dried fruit you like, but make sure they aren't sweetened. And yes, you can add chocolate in these if you'd like to. If you're not a fan of coconut or pumpkin, check out my chocolate chip cookies recipe {see page 184}.

Makes 28 cookies

COCONUT PUMPKIN COOKIES

1 cup almond flour

⅓ cup pumpkin puree

2 large eggs

3 tsp. vanilla extract

1 tsp. cinnamon

½ cup shredded coconut

½ cup raisins

3 Tbsp. melted raw honey

3 Tbsp. melted butter or ghee

a tiny pinch of salt

How-to:

◎ Preheat your oven to 350°F.

◎ Combine all of your ingredients into a large mixing bowl and mix well. The beauty of this recipe is that you don't have to worry about what order it all goes in. Just make sure you crack your eggs first in a separate bowl and then transfer to your large mixing bowl. This will just ensure that you don't have a bad egg and that you don't get shells in your dough.

◎ Get a large cookie sheet out. If it's not a nonstick sheet, line it with aluminum foil. {Heck, I line my nonstick pans with aluminum foil anyway to save on clean up!} Also get a small cup or bowl of water ready to go.

◎ Use a teaspoon to measure out your dough onto the sheet. I do a heaping teaspoon, which means I overfill my teaspoon with cookie dough.

◎ Wet your fingers a little bit with water and spread out the dough so it's a thin even layer {or however thick or thin you want it}. These cookies don't spread out, so you don't have to worry about giving them a lot of space on the sheet.

@ Bake for 8–10 minutes or until golden brown around the edge and underneath. When they're done, let them cool. Plate up and enjoy!

AUTHOR'S NOTE:

These are fantastic slathered in butter or ghee. And as a quick FYI, these cookies aren't crispy. They're a softer cookie, but by making them thinner, they don't turn out as "cakey" as they might otherwise.

These little beauties are dance-worthy. You'll make them, try them, and dance around your kitchen because you're so happy you made them! These truffles are so good, even Mr. Not-So-Paleo will eat them {and he's not a big fan of desserts and sweets}. The fact that he requests these says it all in my book! They might look hard to make because of the length of the directions, but trust me—they are super easy. I explain everything in fine detail so it will be wicked easy for you. I used almond butter in these, but if you've got another favorite nut butter, feel free to use it. Make sure your nut butter is just nuts only and doesn't have any additive ingredients. You also want to make sure the dark chocolate has no soy, is gluten free, and, if possible, has no dairy.

Makes 25 truffles

ALMOND BUTTER TRUFFLES

2 {3.5-oz.} 85% dark chocolate bars
{you could also use chocolate chips}

4 Tbsp. almond butter
{crunchy or smooth}

1 tsp. vanilla extract

½ tsp. cinnamon

unsweetened shredded coconut
{optional}

How-to:

⊚ Create a double boiler to melt your chocolate. To do this, find a heat-safe mixing bowl {I like glass or stainless steel} that will nestle nicely on top, or slightly in, a saucepan. Fill the saucepan halfway with water, place the bowl on top, and turn your heat on medium-low. Let the water start to simmer. Remember, you don't want the water to ever boil—keep it at a constant simmer.

⊚ Chop up 1½ chocolate bars and add to your double boiler to melt. Make sure that you don't have steam coming out the sides of your saucepan and up the bowl. The fastest way to ruin melted chocolate is to get water on or in it!

⊚ Once it's melted, add in your almond butter, vanilla extract, and cinnamon. Stir it around until everything is melted and combined and then turn off the heat. Let it sit for a few minutes to cool down and then use some plastic wrap to cover it. When covering, make sure to press the plastic wrap on top of your mixture so it doesn't form a skin layer.

⊚ Leave the mixture in the fridge until it's hard {normally a few hours}, or you can leave it in there for a few days. Whatever floats your boat!

Directions continue on next page.

- ❦ Take it out of the fridge and let it sit on the counter to warm up for about 10 minutes {unless your kitchen is extra warm, in which case the mixture will warm up faster}.

- ❦ Use a spoon or a small ice cream scoop to scoop out your hardened chocolate. Then roll it into a ball and place on a baking sheet lined with aluminum foil. Continue to do this until all the chocolate is used up. You should end up with around 25 balls. Place the sheet in the fridge

- ❦ Don't put your chocolate bowl in the sink just yet. Set it back up as a double boiler, on medium-low. Chop the remaining half chocolate bar and add it to the double boiler. Why do I have you reuse the bowl? Because it's already flavored from your truffle mixture, saving you an extra dish to wash and giving you great flavor without adding anything extra in!

- ❦ Once your chocolate is melted, pull your truffles out of the fridge. Roll a ball in the melted chocolate. Then use 2 forks to get the ball out and put it back on the sheet. Repeat until all your truffles are coated.

- ❦ If desired, sprinkle on a little bit of shredded coconut.

- ❦ Put them back in the fridge to harden for at least 1 hour. Serve and enjoy!

INDEX

ABOUT THE AUTHOR

Elizabeth McGaw is convinced she was born with a camera in one hand and a chef's knife in the other. She attributes her love of cooking to her father, who taught her everything she knows about preparing a meal. As for her love of photography, she attributes that to the old Polaroid camera she received as a child. Armed with both passions, she created a blog, *Paleo on a Budget*, dedicated to the money-saving side of the paleo lifestyle. She and her husband, dog, and cat reside in Concord, New Hampshire, where they can be found photographing weddings for fun and building websites.

You can learn more about Liz and her blog at

www.paleoonabudget.com